IMAGINING THE ROMAN EMPIRE

Essays on Travel & Antiquity in the Mediterranean

IMAGINING THE ROMAN EMPIRE

Essays on Travel & Antiquity in the Mediterranean

By Zoë Tavares Bennett & Grace DeAngelis

MEDITERRA
PRESS

To the Intercollegiate Center for Classical Studies,

where we first traveled back in time,

and to our families,

who keep us anchored in the present.

ὁμοίως σμικρὰ καὶ μεγάλα ἄστεα ἀνθρώπων ἐπεξιών. τὰ γὰρ τὸ πάλαι μεγάλα ἦν, τὰ πολλὰ σμικρὰ αὐτῶν γέγονε: τὰ δὲ ἐπ' ἐμεῦ ἦν μεγάλα, πρότερον ἦν σμικρά. τὴν ἀνθρωπηίην ὦν ἐπιστάμενος εὐδαιμονίην οὐδαμὰ ἐν τὠυτῷ μένουσαν, ἐπιμνήσομαι ἀμφοτέρων ὁμοίως.

I will cover minor and major human cities equally, because most of those which were great in the past have become small by now, and those which were great in my own time were small in times past. I will mention both equally because I know that human happiness never remains long in the same place.

—Herodotus, *The Histories, 1.5.4*

Nescire autem quid ante quam natus sis acciderit, id est semper esse puerum. Quid enim est aetas hominis, nisi ea memoria rerum veterum cum superiorum aetate contexitur?

Moreover, not to know what happened before you were born is to be always a child. For what is a man's life worth, unless by the memory of ancient deeds it is interwoven with the life of our ancestors?

—Cicero, *Orator 120*

How wonderful it must have been to Ulysses to venture into this Mediterranean and open his eyes on all the loveliness of the tall coasts. How marvellous to steal with his ship into these magic harbours. There is something eternally morning-glamorous about these lands as they rise from the sea. And it is always the Odyssey which comes back to one as one looks at them. All the lovely morning-wonder of this world, in Homer's day!

—D.H. Lawrence, *Sea and Sardinia*

CONTENTS

MEDIA

INTRODUCTION

FOUR COUNTRIES, TWO TRAVELERS, one month, ten essays. We don't consider ourselves scholarly experts, travel gurus, or essayists by nature. We are students of the Classical world, and with both passion and hubris, we set out one summer on a long and arduous journey throughout the Ancient Mediterranean.

Our desire to cross the grand territory of the Roman Empire and document our travels in words arose somewhat accidentally. We only wished to blog and photograph our trip for family and friends, but our investigation into the past and present of each archeological site we visited turned into a more intense and perilous quest than we had expected.

After all, time-traveling is not for the faint of heart. Buried beside the ruins of these ancient and sacred sites lay the remains of those who lived long before us, traces of them visible in the very rock and stone through which we picked a very old path. Trying to untangle the centuries of history from the ground, from shadows and memories now long forgotten, proved more difficult than we could have imagined. Even many months after our trip came to an end, the heavy burden of more than a millennia has stayed with us.

Only two thousand years ago—a mere breath in the history of humanity—the Roman Empire spanned from the Western shores of Portugal to the edges of India in the east, and from the borders of Ethiopia in the south to Britain in the north. Our goal to cover the entire Empire in our travels was more of a dream than reality; in truth, we would hardly brush the surface of its once far-reaching territory, visiting a handful of cities and attempting to reimagine its full weight and texture from a few meager scraps.

However, the few places we did reach were remarkably beautiful and vibrant with life, both then and now. Some have been extolled for centuries, others are obliviously left on the wayside. All of them hold memory. We understood early on that our pens were recorders not of facts or events, but of truth, that subtle, malleable substance that shines forth from the past like sunlight through a crack in rock. Truth is where present and past mingle, like song and myth once did in poetry, so that one might glimpse Clytemnestra lingering atop her crumbling acropolis or Odysseus and his ship dipping beneath the waves of a wine-dark sea.

In the ancient world, the travel alone for this trip would take 99.23 days or about 3.2 months according to Stanford's ORBIS. If we add the roughly 28 days of pure sightseeing and walking around each city—not to mention the public transit we used, which would add more days of travel—this would make our trip in the ancient world last a total of over 4 months. Thanks to modern methods of transportation, however, we flew into Lisbon and began our trip on July 1st, 2023, ending a mere month later on August 2nd, 2023.

After touring Lisbon's ancient and modern sites, we took a day trip to Sintra to see her castles and then to Coimbra to see the ancient ruins of Conímbriga. From there we trained down to Evora for a day, hopped on a bus to Mérida across the Spanish border, trained to Seville, and then flew back to Lisbon all in the span of three days.

We then flew to Rome, the heart of the Empire, where we visited our usual haunts, including Ostia Antica and Palestrina. From there we trained to the ancient sites of Baiae and Puteoli for their warm water and cooler weather. A day later we visited Naples for her famed archeological museum and Pompeii, our final destination in Italy before flying to Athens.

Greece embraced us during the hottest week of summer as we toured the mainland, peninsula, and island of Aegina. Besides Athens, we visited ancient sites in Thebes, Delphi, Olympia, Nafplio, and a few others in between, and ended at the seaward-gazing temple of Poseidon at Sounio, where we watched the sun set and the full moon rise on the last day of our trip.

Our recollections and reflections along the way span everything from history to myth to day-to-day musings, and include all of our serious and not-so-serious thoughts about the modern and ancient worlds. This grand adventure attempts to record all the shades and colors of these sites, along with our perilous dives into the depths of the sea, drives along the cliffsides of mountains, and wanderings into forests and fields both magical and dangerous. Accompanying these writings are maps and photos meant to add visual lines and color where we thought the words needed them most.

These essays are for you, dear reader, to join us in this long journey across the Roman Empire, but also to reflect on your own visitations to the past, and what—or who—we may find there. For written history always leaves room for those brave enough to tread her uncharted waves, and as we walk in the footsteps of those who came before us, reflected even in the eyes of the stillest statues or the most ancient of ruins, we might just discover ourselves.

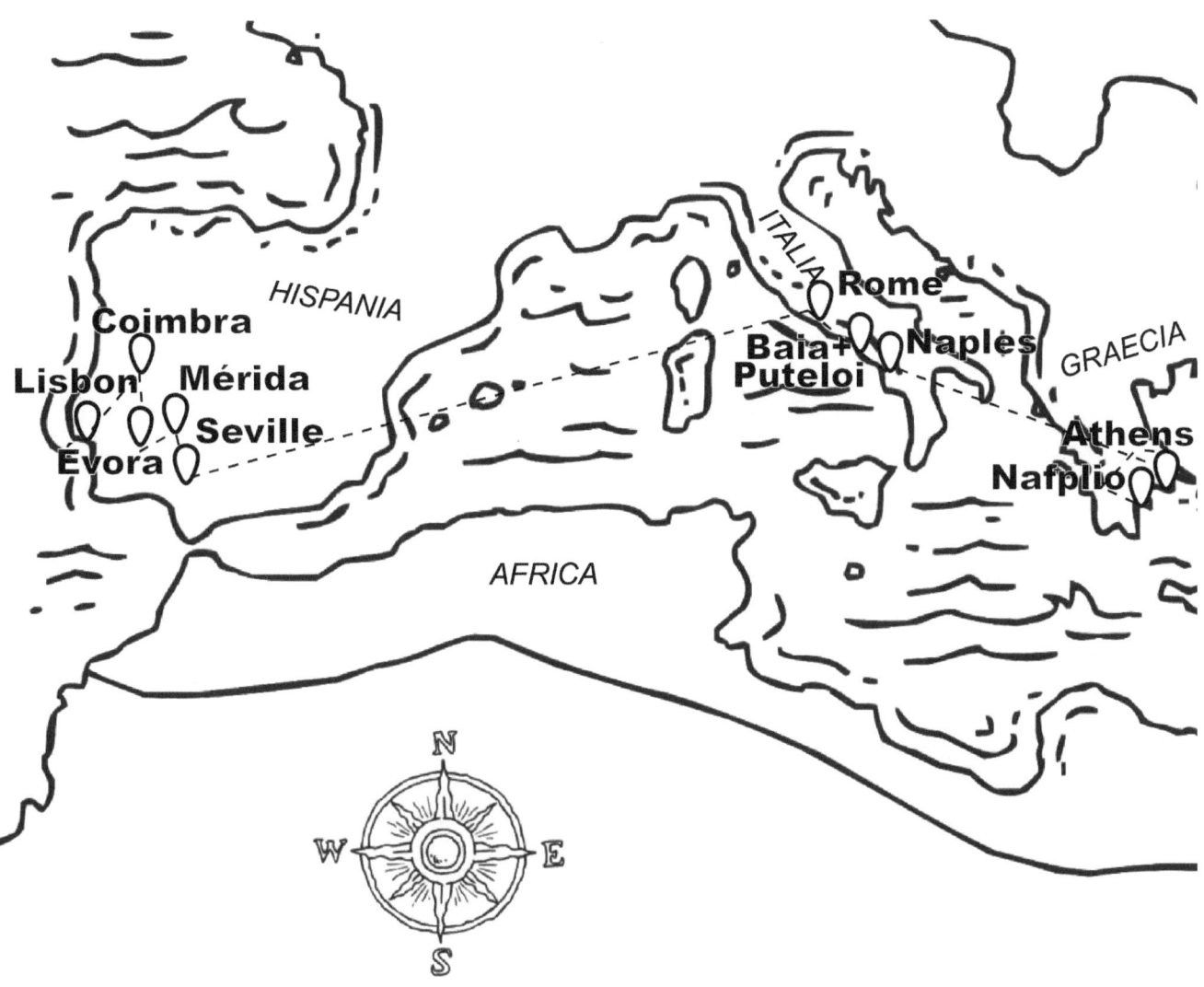

Map of Trip

LISBOA

A Story of Man & Sea

By day Lisbon has a naive theatrical quality that enchants and captivates, but by night it is a fairy-tale city, descending over lighted terraces to the sea, like a woman in festive garments going down to meet her dark lover.
–Erich Maria Remarque

And to the immense and attainable ocean
These shields, which you see here, tell,
That the sea with an end may be Greek or Roman:
The sea without end is Portuguese.
—"Standard," Message, Fernando Pessoa

THE CLIMB UP TO Castelo de São Jorge is steep and slow in the July heat. Rome is not the only city born among seven hills. Lisbon, too, was built on seven hills—São Jorge being one of them—that would rival Rome in their height and command over the river Tagus. But the Tagus, unlike the seagreen waters of Rome's Tiber, is wide and deep like the ocean, filled with fish and oysters which would shape the people who would come to call those hills their home.

Although Lisbon ultimately fell under Roman rule and learned the Latin tongue which binds all Romance languages, there lies a long, rich history of the indigenous Iberians before their language became lost. Legend says that Lisbon was founded by Odysseus—quite fittingly, as a man of the sea—but archeological study shows that there have been permanent settlements of indigenous Iberian people since 2500 BC. Evidence of Iron Age habitation lies buried beneath the Castelo do São Jorge and other parts of the city. A small bronze figurine of a deer, a bird perched on its back, came from this time, revealing artistic sensibility in the barest of remains.

1.1. Small bronze figurine of deer and bird

When the Phoenicians and Greeks established trading posts in Lisbon, the Attic vases and Eastern-style pottery came with them. Many fragments discovered in the area of the Teatro Romano reveal that the inhabitants of Lisbon used pottery not only for decorative but also utilitarian purposes. For example, there are Iron Age amphorae with painted geometric designs still preserved, as well as some that once contained products like *garum*—a popular fish paste—and bear a stamp of the producer's name.

The river Tagus and the sea have connected Lisbon with the rest of the Mediterranean world since its very beginnings. By the time the Romans conquered what was then called Olissipo, the Iberians were already incorporated into a vast empire, not only importing popular Italian cutlery, Greek immigrants, and Eastern influences, but also *exporting*—which they still do to this day—the fruits of the sea and land, such as fish, olive oil, and wine.

Fish, in particular, is a cornerstone of Portuguese culture, especially for those who live on the coast. Codfish (or *bacalhau* in Portuguese), one of the most popular fish to eat, can be cooked in over 365 ways. Sardines can be found today not only in every restaurant and market but also drawn on tiles and mosaics and sewn onto handbags and clothing. The love of the sea is ingrained in every aspect of life: the stacked buildings face longingly towards the water, going to the beach is as habitual as taking a stroll, and even the city itself seems to slip into the water, with the stone quay of Cais das Colunas a bridge between land and sea.

1.2 Cais das Colunas

The importance of fish in Portugal today is a reflection of the role it held in ancient Olissipo. The city was one of the main producers of *garum* for the Roman Empire. Several *garum* factories were established along the river for easy access to the necessary supply of fish and salt. The ruins of one such factory have been preserved on the first floor of the Casa dos Bicos, where we see the massive vats in which the makers would layer fish and salt before allowing the mixture to ferment and liquify. The inhabitants of Olissipo exported *garum* all over the Mediterranean world, even to locations as far away as present-day Syria. Though people in antiquity considered it a delicacy, *garum*—perhaps for the best—no longer holds a place in modern cuisine.

Even the Romans understood the importance of the sea to the native people of Lisbon. When Emperor Augustus in the early first century CE commissioned the theater whose ruins still stand today, he chose the more expensive and labor-intensive terracing on a high hill so that the theater would face the water. This was not only to strengthen the image of the Roman Empire but also to give power to the people. In fact, the theater was open to everyone, rich or poor, free or enslaved.

We feel this same inclusivity when we visit the Museum of the Roman Theater, which costs a mere 3 euros for entrance into both the museum and the archeological site on the ground floor of the Casa dos Bicos. As we descend the staircase of the museum to an open-air layer, which has been dug into the earth with glass walkways built to give museum goers a better look at the site, we discover a mirror and a pile of cloth at the end of the walkway. There are step-by-step instructions written beside the mirror on how to put on a *palla*, the Roman woman's shawl that would be wrapped around her dress. We gleefully record ourselves wrapping the fabrics around our waists and over our left shoulders, posing in the mirror and, for a moment, feeling like true Romans of Olissipo.

Interestingly, archaeologists discovered a huge amount of stone fishing weights when they excavated the foundations of the theater. About half the size of a brick, these weights are a surprising find (not being the most natural building material) but a logical one nonetheless: considering the widespread importance of fishing in Olissipo, these weights must have been so prevalent and common that the townspeople had extras to spare for building. Even in the construction of their theater, it seems, they found a way to involve the sea.

The Romans, however, were not the only people to conquer Lisbon, and once the empire fell, countless other powerful armies would occupy the city and leave their own traces behind. After several Iranian and Germanic tribes invaded Lisbon, in 711 the Muslim forces of the Umayyad Caliphate occupied the city and built many mosques, a castle (now the Castelo de São Jorge), and other buildings, as well as a new method of irrigated agriculture. The name for Alfama, the oldest district of Lisbon, derives from the Arabic *"al-hamma"* (meaning "hot springs" or "fountains"), and the Portuguese language today has over 600 loan words from Arabic.

Despite the many centuries of rule under foreign powers, a devastating earthquake, tsunami, and fire that destroyed the city in 1755, and the longest-lived fascist dictatorship in Western Europe, the people of Lisbon have always persisted. Their native Iberian language may have long ago disappeared, but some things have remained the same, like the Tagus River ever-flowing into the open sea. Everything from the black and white mosaics on the cobblestone streets to the colorful buildings roofed in orange, some with walls entirely covered in intricate tile work of blue and yellow and green, mirror the city and its patchwork of history, open to all people but still prideful, still very much Portuguese.

1.3 Fishing weights

On a whim, we decide to drive to Óbidos, a small town about an hour north of Lisbon. The name "Óbidos" derives from the Latin word *oppidum*, a term referring specifically to towns with fortification walls. Óbidos itself does not seem to have been a Roman town, though some Roman-era ruins have been discovered in the area which are related to the nearby Roman (and previously Celtic) settlement of Eburobrittium. What makes Óbidos interesting today is—rather appropriately to its name—the survival of the medieval castle walls that surround the town. The castle was first built in the 8th century by Muslim occupants, but the Portuguese kings who ruled Óbidos from the 12th century onwards continually augmented and remodeled the structure.

Óbidos looks like how one might imagine Lisbon did when fortified stone walls still encircled the city, with houses stacked upon one another, surrounded by agricultural land and green hills. Every year in late July, Óbidos holds an extravagant Medieval festival, keeping old Portuguese traditions alive in a new world. Yet the quiet farms we pass on our drive back and the fishermen on their boats out at sea suggest that the important things, at least, have not really changed at all.

1.4 Rua do Alecrim in Lisbon

SINTRA

THE PRINCESS & THE PEASANT

In the bay of the arch, as inside a heavy stone frame, shone the rich afternoon light, a marvellous picture of almost fantastic composition, like the illustration of a beautiful legend of chivalry and love. In the foreground was the courtyard, deserted and growing green, all speckled with yellow buds; in the background the serried row of ancient trees, with ivy on their trunks, forming a wall of glittering foliage along the frame. Emerging abruptly from this leafy line of sunny copse, one climbed into the full splendour of the day, in which, standing out vigorously in clear relief against the bright blue sky, was the airy summit of the mountains, all dark violet and crowned by the Pena Palace, romantic and solitary on high, with its dark park at its feet, the slender tower lost in the air and the domes shining in the sun as if made of gold...
—Eça de Queiróz, *The Tragedy of Rua das Flores*

Today is the happiest day of my life. I know Italy, Sicily, Greece and Egypt, and I have never seen anything, anything, to match the Pena. It is the most beautiful thing I have ever seen. This is the true Garden of Klingsor and there, up above, is the Castle of the Holy Grail.
—Richard Strauss

THE RIDE UP TO the palaces of Sintra is terrifying. Our bus hurdles around tight pin-curves up the steep mountainside, narrowly dodging tourists who have foregone the 15€ all-day bus ticket in favor of the grueling hike up the mountain. The streets are cobblestoned, with a high stone wall on one side and a sheer cliff on the other, and the bus rattles and screeches in protest. It reminds us that this road was never built with cars and buses in mind, but rather was meant for a long and arduous journey by horse and carriage, or else simply on foot.

We imagine that, five hundred years ago, we would have taken a carriage up to the palace, which perhaps would have been more comfortable than standing in a crowded, humid bus. But as private cars and small three-wheel tourist carts zoom past our bus on its third stop, we realize that we actually would not have been in the horse-drawn carriage—in fact, if we were not hiking up the mountain as a peasant in service to the king, we probably would not have come up the mountain at all.

But the views alone are worth the slightly perilous trip up. With the mist shrouding the mountain range, it is easy to see why Columella, a first-century CE Roman writer, called it *Sacer Mons Hispaniae*, or "the sacred mountain of Hispania" (*De Re Rustica* 6.27.7). Actually, the Romans were not the only ones to find the deep green, forested mountains of Sintra compelling. Sintra has been occupied since the Paleolithic era and felt Roman influence beginning in the 2nd/1st centuries BCE. It was part of the territory of the Roman town of Olissipo, with a well-trodden road connecting them.

In the 8th century, while in control of the Iberian peninsula, Muslim rulers built a castle in the Sintra Mountains, the spectacular ruins of which still stand today as the Castelo dos Mouros ("Castle of the Moors"). Following the Christians' capture of Sintra, the city was ruled by a variety of royal dynasties until the establishment of the Portuguese Republic in 1910.

Due to the massive lines of tourists, our trip begins on lower ground at the Quinta da Regaleira (which translates to "the estate of Regaleira"). Originally belonging to the Regaleira noble family, Carvalho Monteiro purchased the land in 1892 and constructed a palace in addition to expansive luxury gardens with winding paths, hidden tunnels, and verdant greenery.

As we walk around the Quinta's dizzying paths and bridges and underground labyrinths, there is the sense that we are meant to get lost, as if the line between manicured garden and untamed nature grows thin as we lose all sense of direction in the damp tunnels of connecting caves beneath the park, where even the flashlight on our phones can hardly light our path in the darkness.

But despite the nearly boundless nature in the gardens, once inside the palace, there is no mistaking who held dominion over every inch of the property. The refinement of each room in the palace strikes immediately upon entering; the juxtaposition of the palace's sophistication against the sense of wilderness suggested by the gardens underscores Monteiro's power over not just his residence but also over nature itself.

The Quinta is reminiscent of ancient Roman villa estates, where the elite owners dedicated significant swaths of the grounds to plantings and walking paths while also demonstrating their wealth and social status through elegant architecture and decoration in both the constructed and natural spaces of their estates. The palace itself is full of Classical influence, from statuary to design motifs to Latin quotations adorning the walls. The quote *'De gustibus non est disputandum'*—meaning "on matters of taste, there can be no discussion"—in the dining room is a particular favorite of ours.

2.1 Quinta da Regaleira

After our strolls of the Quinta da Regaleira have come to an end, we hop on the bus that will bring us—after inexplicable traffic—to the final stop and grand finale: the Palácio da Pena. The palace was first built as a monastery in the 15th century but abandoned after the 1755 Lisbon earthquake. In 1838, the King Consort Ferdinand II bought the ruins and transformed them into the stunning royal structures that stand today in their unmistakable reds, yellows, and blues.

After the death of Ferdinand, the palace came into the possession of his second wife, the Countess of Edla, whose correspondences by letter in French—Ferdinand even addresses the countess as *Chéri*—are on display in the palace. She ultimately sold the palace in 1889 to King Luís for use by the royal family, and after the Republican Revolution of 1910 it was transformed into a museum. Queen Amélia, the last queen of Portugal who outlived both husband and children, spent her last night at the palace before going into exile.

Even as a museum, the palace invites us in as much as it intimidates, and the laborious hike from the ticket booth to the entrance of the palace itself reminds us that the towering red turrets and grand blue and yellow arches and terraces were not built for mere commoners like us. However, despite being herded in a long, Disneyland-esque line through the rooms of the palace, it is difficult to feel anything but admiration for the breathtaking architecture and tiled walls, the ornate and intricate furniture, and the gold and silver accents of each space.

But it is the unending view from the Queen's terrace of evergreen mountains cloaked in fog that makes it all worth it. This is a view fit for royalty, and perhaps that is the gift of our time—that, for a moment, regardless of the struggle it has taken to climb up and stand atop a centuries-old palace, we know then what it feels like to be queen.

2.2 Palácio da Pena

CONÍMBRIGA & COIMBRA

A Tale of Two Cities

The only thing that matters is to feel the fado. The fado is not meant to be sung; it simply happens. You feel it, you don't understand it and you don't explain it.
– Amália Rodrigues

There is, in the westernmost part of Iberia, a very strange people: they neither govern themselves nor allow themselves to be governed!
–Portugese saying, often attributed to Julius Caesar

EARLY WEDNESDAY MORNING, WE hop on the first of only two buses that would journey to the Conímbriga ruins that day, an archeological site about eleven miles outside the modern city of Coimbra. The bus drops us off outside the museum in a beautiful courtyard with trees and a large garden pool. We follow the winding dirt path to the extensive grounds of the site and find ourselves at a luxury Roman bath complex.

We descend a staircase below the Greek-style palestra—a wide open space used for exercise and teaching—and, to our complete and utter surprise, encounter foundational ruins of the indigenous Iberians from the 4th century BCE.

Even though we often consider Greek and Roman civilizations to be the "beginning" of Western culture, in places such as Portugal and Spain, the Romans were, in fact, conquerors. Conímbriga stands as proof that, long before the expanding Roman empire subsumed the Iberian peninsula, there was an established culture and civilization already living there for several hundred years. These foundational ruins sit beneath the bath complex that the Romans built on top of them, overlooking a lush green valley peppered with slanting gray rock, a winding river somewhere down below.

3.1 View from ancient site of Conímbriga

As we stare at the view that these indigenous Iberians had surely admired too, in the near silence the sounds of the forest seem to come from all around, and we cannot help but wonder how much louder the humming and chirping would have sounded six thousand years ago. Conímbriga, fittingly, comes from the indigenous words *conim*, "the place of rocky eminence," and *briga*, a suffix meaning "citadel." The citadel they are referring to is hard to glimpse among the dominant Roman ruins, but fortunately what remains of the indigenous community reveals some intriguing insights as to the lives they led before and after the Roman conquest.

Remains of the indigenous town lie underneath the bath complex, the forum, and some of the later Roman-era houses. Several houses cluster around a shared central patio with terraces that overlook it, suggesting that even domestic life was deeply rooted in the wider community. The surviving traces of their roads—including roads that paralleled each other or intersected at right angles—demonstrate that the town was laid out according to a specific, predetermined plan rather than a random smattering of houses. This plan, however, differed from the later Roman street map. The evidence is unmistakeable, right before our eyes and beneath our feet: prior to the Romans' arrival in Conímbriga, an indigenous community had already established itself as a town.

But as we wander through the residential areas of ancient Conímbriga, even the layout of the Roman-era houses strikes us as quite different from what we have previously seen at archaeological sites in Italy. The stereotypical Italic Roman house is laid out along a central axis, with a line of sight from the entrance—passing through the middle of the house's interior courtyard and the *tablinum* (a sort of office)—to a second garden space at the back of the house. But in the ruins of houses that we observe in Conímbriga, the sightline of the domestic spaces ends at the *triclinium* (dining room), which would traditionally be off to the side in an Italic Roman house.

Considering this difference, it seems that not only did the indigenous Iberians adapt to the customs and culture of the Romans, but the Romans, too, were influenced by the Iberian people, laying the foundations for the culture today that is uniquely Portuguese. Perhaps it is no surprise that the dining room would hold center stage in a Hispanic-Roman household when sitting down every day for a three-course lunch ("almoço") and dinner ("jantar") are at the heart of Portuguese daily life today.

Yet we could not help but admire the Roman villas of the new Conímbriga elite. One of the most spectacular elements of the archaeological site is the House of the Fountains (*Casa dos Repuxos* in Portuguese), a luxurious and large domestic space dating to the 2nd century AD. Archaeologists gave the house this name because its interior courtyard contains a pool surrounded by over five hundred water jets, a unique and impressive feat for the ancient world. The site's curators have made the jets functional, meaning that we are able to see them turn on and pour thin streams of water into the pool. Hearing the gentle splashing of the fountains and gazing upon the intricate mosaics of mythological scenes adorning the courtyard's floors (our favorite being the Minotaur's labyrinth), we feel as though we are Roman women relaxing and enjoying a summer's day by the fountain.

3.2 Casa dos Repuxos

Even though the Romans of the Imperial era (31 BC – AD 476) built a large fortified wall along one side of the town—whose towering remains today seem to foreshadow typical medieval castle walls—by the Middle Ages, the seat of political, cultural, and religious power had moved from Conímbriga to the city that is now called Coimbra.

Although one would not suspect it from wandering through the streets of modern day Coimbra, underneath the buildings lies the ancient Roman town of Aeminium. We are able to venture into Coimbra's Roman past at the Museu Machado de Castro, which stands on the former site of the forum. The forum was located on the slope of a hill, so the Romans constructed a cryptoporticus to support it—whose hallways we are able to walk through!—and to allow the forum's flat horizontal surface to stand on an artificial platform.

The stone cryptoporticus has windows to let in some light, which also provide a gorgeous view over the city and mountains. Walking through the ancient cryptoporticus, we are reminded that Coimbra, which features so many cultural institutions significant in the present day, is supported by its history as a Roman city.

This Roman presence permeates its neighboring institution, the University of Coimbra. Founded originally in Lisbon in 1290, it is the oldest university of Portugal. As literary and Catholic influence shifted to Coimbra, the university was relocated there in 1308, increasing its status as the cultural epicenter of Portugal. Built on the grounds of a former palace—in whose throne room current students actually deliver their Ph.D. defenses—the university commands a grand view of the valleys and river below from an expansive courtyard lined with Classically-inspired buildings.

3.3 University of Coimbra

Beside the palace is the Chapel of São Miguel, whose interior walls are filled from top to bottom with characteristic *azulejos*—tiles traditionally decorated in blue and white—and which reminds us of Portugal's history and influence from Arabo-Hispanic aesthetics and culture. In its conception, *azulejos* featured Islamic, Gothic, and Renaissance motifs and would later include themes of Classical antiquity. They would even be used as teaching tools for mathematical principles. In many ways, *azulejos* are a symbolic example of continuity in time as well as cultural exchange across the Mediterranean.

3.4 Azulejo with mathematical formulae

Despite the beauty of the palace and chapel, particularly stunning is the University's Biblioteca Joanina, a Baroque-style construction that is one of the most beautiful libraries in the world and contains over 200,000 volumes of 16th–18th century literary works.

As we ascend the steps to its third floor, we are not allowed to take photos, and we have only ten minutes to glimpse at the shelves upon shelves of books encased in elaborate wood and gold. It is like walking into a world in which the lives of ancient Romans were mere moments ago, accessible if only we could reach out and turn one of those delicate pages. On the wall above the entrance doors, an inscription in Latin reads:

Panduntur cunctis exculta Palatia libris:
Huc ades, auctores consule, doctus eris.
Haec tibi pro studiis et lex et norma tenenda est:
Mens legat, observet sedula, penna notet.

The palace, adorned with books, is open to all:
Come here, consult the authors—you will be educated.
For your studies, you must uphold this law and precept:
Let your mind read and observe diligently; let your pen take notes.

Coimbra and its educational and religious influence have faded since its height of power, but as we walk the streets at night—previously crowded by an antique book fair and festival—we see evidence of the city's cultural heritage at every corner. Down the road we hear the traditional Fado songs tenderly sung, accompanied by the teardrop-shaped Portuguese *guitarra*. Fado are typically mournful songs about *saudade*, an untranslatable word in Portuguese that can be described as an intense feeling of longing, perhaps for the past or a loved one at sea.

As we end our last night with good food and glasses of sangria, we discuss plans of the future and the momentariness of the present, when all too soon we begin reminiscing about different times and places, reliving fond memories. It seems the delicate notes drifting down the street remind us that the past, after all, is more like memory, and it is only through us that it remains alive in the present.

ÉVORA

History Set in Stone

Before the curtains of history lifted, one feels the world was like this—this Celtic bareness and sombreness and air. But perhaps it is not Celtic at all: Iberian. Nothing is more unsatisfactory than our conception of what is Celtic and what is not Celtic. I believe there were never any Celts, as a race.—As for Iberians—!
—D.H. Lawrence, *Sea and Sardinia*

The city of Évora sits in the valley of Alentejo, one of the driest regions of Portugal. But the rolling hills filled with cork and holm oak trees have ancient, secret ways of surviving the hot summer months, sharing water and nutrients beneath the soil, a web of roads which bear messages to the roots of every plant and tree.

We humans, too, long ago discovered the abundance of this land. As a period of global warming melted the glaciers around 10,000 years ago, humans sailed down the rivers that nourish this region, domesticating plants and animals, like the black pig, a unique free-range pig found only on the Iberian Peninsula and which makes a very tasty dinner. Unlike the pink-skinned pigs we are used to, the pigs of this region developed more melanin from eating the fruit of the surrounding oak trees: acorns. They used the fire resistant and waterproof cork as insulation and clothing. They used the holm oak as slow-burning logs for fire. And it was also around this time, as early as 9000 years ago, that they began to build. They did not simply build houses, or roads, or towns—those had already existed for a long time. No, they started building something that would last, something that they hoped would stand for an eternity.

Our Ébora Megalithic tour guide, Sira, picks us up outside our hotel to drive us to see the Neolithic ruins. To Classicists, the Neolithic age (10000–4500 BC) can seem a far-off whisper from the grand civilizations of Greece and Italy that we study. When we imagine the Neolithic age, we envision thatched huts and spears and crude pottery. We might even think of hunter-gatherers, or cavemen in loincloths. But by the time humans reached Évora, they were already sedentary. In fact, they would be much more familiar to us than we realize, and if we were to see them as they herded their animals with a curved staff or plowed their fields, we would simply call them farmers and shepherds.

As Sira drives us beyond the modern city of Évora, we steadily ascend to the top of the hills. We pass farms with beautiful white and black cows, walking single-file to be milked, a few of them very round and pregnant. The van makes the laborious journey up the dirt road until we reach a clearing at the top of a hill. On the slope are tall, rounded stones—called *menhirs*—stuck in the ground vertically, forming a long, oval-shaped ring.

This is not the first cromlech, as such rock formations are called, to have been made. Countless others, as ancient as 9000 years old, have been found in Portugal, let alone throughout the rest of the world. But these are not just random stones placed in the ground. They are not just markers of a gathering space or even artistic monuments, though they certainly bear symbols and meanings themselves. These stones point to something greater.

The first cromlechs ever built were comprised of *menhirs*, the elongated stones, in rows upon rows of straight lines. It was only about 2000 years later that the cromlechs such as the one we are seeing, called the Cromlech of Almendres, began to appear. In the grand scheme of history, 2000 years may not seem like a long time, but as Sira pointed out to us, "That's us compared to the Romans." And as Classicists know very well, entire civilizations can rise and fall within 2000 years. When the next wave of cromlechs were made, they were no longer set in rows as the previous civilization had done, but follow two specific rules that can be observed in every cromlech on the archeological record: 1) the stones make a semicircle or horseshoe shape, and 2) they are built on a slope, facing east and the rising sun.

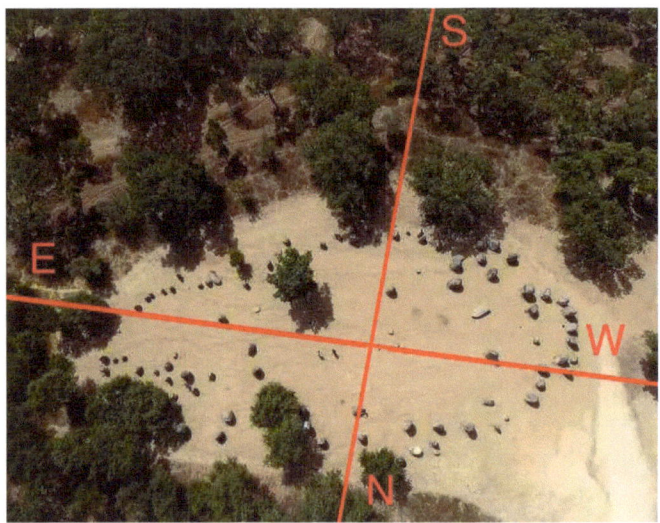

4.1 Overhead map of the Cromlech of Almendres with cardinal directions

The cromlech, at its heart, is two large menhirs aligned on the same east-west axis. This is no coincidence. Our Neolithic ancestors did not idly watch the stars; they were carefully tracking the movements of the heavens in order to know things that we take for granted in our modern daily lives, like the precise point on the horizon where the sun will set on any given day. But for farmers and shepherds, these calculations were vital for survival, indicating essential knowledge like when to plant and when to harvest.

In fact, these stones did not just point east. They also measured the summer and winter solstices on the north-south axis, as well as the spring and fall equinoxes. They followed not only the cycle of the moon from new to full, but also its Metonic cycle, when the phases of the moon recur on the same days of the solar year, a cycle only completed every 19 years. These stones might measure things which our clocks and phones do easily, but they also point to important days of the year which we still consider sacred today, though we do not always realize it. Perhaps, just like us, the Neolithic peoples celebrated the coming of the seasons, and if we were to go back in time on the spring equinox, their celebration would not look so very different to a Christian Easter.

Yet here begins the biggest mystery of all. For these stones were not simply built to track the movements of the heavens—these people have known the right times to plant and harvest for generations. It was not *need* that drove them to build these monuments, but *want*. There are many theories as to why they built these monuments. Could it have served as a gathering space? Could it have even been a kind of theater, a semicircle centered on one person upon whom the evening sun would shine? Or could it have represented their elders—now turned to stone—begging the sun to rise, as so many ancient stories tell?

Although the *why* of these monuments may be difficult to answer, as we gaze upon the eastern horizon, the modern Évora in the valley below, her famous Gothic Cathedral still visible from miles away, we realize that the answer might be something closer to home, something more familiar, something, we think, more human. For it would be another 6000 years before a very different civilization built their own impressive stone monument in the Alentejo region, this one at the heart of the medieval town of Évora. The *Sé de Évora* (Portuguese for 'Cathedral of Évora') is not only the highest lookout point in the city but the largest medieval cathedral in all of Portugal. Before climbing over a hundred stairs to the top, we walk around the cathedral's cloister, a courtyard that seems straight out of a Harry Potter movie. From the top of the cathedral, we behold a panoramic view of Évora and the surrounding agricultural land.

Adjacent to the cathedral and easily visible from the cathedral's lookout-point stands the gleaming 'Temple of Diana,' constructed in the first century CE. (Though the temple is today often said to be 'of Diana,' archaeologists think that it may in fact have been dedicated to the Roman imperial cult.) Along with the temple, the small open square and surrounding buildings—including the Museu Frei Manuel do Cenáculo, housing Neolithic and Roman artifacts—once formed the site of the ancient forum.

Évora became a Roman town in 57 BCE, when it was conquered by Julius Caesar and given the name of *Liberalitas Julia* ('Julian Generosity'). The town was especially important for its role in the empire's wheat and silver trade and became prominent within the province of Hispania. Walking through Évora, it is striking that many aspects of the city's past have continued to be central in its present day. Its buildings still retain a sense of artistic unity as their Roman predecessors did, sharing a common aesthetic of whitewashed walls, windows bordered by yellow, and doors painted green. Nearly all of the souvenir shops lining the streets display shelves upon shelves of products made from cork, testifying to the essential role that this material has played in shaping Évora's development since its Neolithic beginnings.

4.2 Cromlech of Almendre

Évora's contemporary architecture also echoes the Neolithic cromlechs. The heart of the present-day community is the Praça do Giraldo, which, being ovular in shape, allows for and even encourages the same type of public gatherings, celebrations, and communal living as the cromlechs did millenia ago. Gazing over the rooftops and the remnants of the Roman-era wall that once surrounded the city, it is easy to imagine Évora as it was 2000 years in the past. Ultimately, the grand Cathedral, the stately Roman temple, and the evocative cromlech were all built by different people in very different times, yet they still stand today, their strong stones meant to last.

Our tour of the Neolithic ruins ends with another massive stone structure. Two thousand years after the creation of the cromlechs—the rise and fall of yet another civilization—emerges the dolmen, a funerary monument consisting of a long passageway leading into a round burial chamber, with stone slabs as walls and one giant capstone as a roof. Archaeologists have discovered over two thousand dolmens dating to the Neolithic period, but the 'Anta Grande do Zambujeiro', which we are visiting today, is one of the largest ever found. Located about 7 miles outside of modern-day Évora, it was constructed approximately 5000 years ago.

4.3 Anta Grande do Zambujeiro, missing capstone and facing east

When it was first constructed, the entire dolmen was covered with earth so that it would appear as no more than a hill from the outside, though the footsteps of archeologists and tourists have since eroded the dirt away. Anywhere from one or two to more than thirty people could be entombed in a single dolmen depending on its size—which of course, depended on wealth. Those who buried the dead also placed objects necessary for survival and daily life, such as sewing needles, cookware, and arrowheads, suggesting that the Neolithic peoples believed in some sort of afterlife or resurrection. But, just as we think we are coming to understand these tombs and these people, we learn the most mysterious thing of all.

The dolmens discovered in Portugal, says Sira, all have their entrances pointing towards the east, just as the cromlechs. However, the dolmens do not consistently point due east—and no, this is not on account of mis-calculation. Their orientations vary only within a strict 30 degree angle due east. This corresponds *exactly* to the range where the first full moon after the spring equinox appears on the horizon during the moon's metonic—or 19 year—cycle. In other words, when burying their dead, they aligned their tombs specifically to the spring equinox and the full moon, symbols that have long been associated with renewal, resurrection, and fertility. Is it a coincidence that the bodies in dolmens were consistently placed in the fetal position?

"Maybe the dolmen represents pregnancy!" Grace exclaims. "The chamber is the womb, the entryway is the birth canal, the hill of dirt is like a woman's pregnant stomach, and the people are in fetal position so they can be reborn."

Sira smiles at us. "Maybe. You wouldn't be the first to think that."

Perhaps there will never be a way to answer the question of why these monuments were made, or what beliefs the Neolithic peoples held about the sun and moon. But that's the thing, right? These monuments all have one thing in common, and it has to do with the earth that their stones came from, the wonder we feel as we look upon them, and the questions we then ask ourselves. Studying history, after all, is really just a convoluted, complicated, and often tedious way of answering a very old and simple question: what does it mean to be human?

And as we gaze upon the same eastern horizon where people several thousand years ago watched—maybe even begged—for the sun to rise, we realize that the very *why* that we ask of the universe, about life and death and life after death, is ultimately what makes us human, whether in this civilization or the next. Perhaps this tombstone engraving for a Roman woman named Nice says it best:

Whoever you are, wanderer, who passes by me, buried in this place, if you pity me—after you have read that I died on my twentieth year of life—and if my rest moves you, I shall pray that you, when weary, may have a sweeter rest, a longer life and a slow aging in this life, which I was not permitted to enjoy. Crying will not suit you. Why won't you enjoy the years? Inachus and Io made this monument for me. Go, it's preferable; haste thee, now that you have read what you had to read. Go. Nice lived twenty years.

—Tombstone of Nice, found in Évora

4.4. Temple of Diana

MÉRIDA & SEVILLE

CROSSROADS OF WORLDS OLD AND NEW

There is no nightlife in Spain. They stay up late but they get up late. That is not nightlife. That is delaying the day.
– Ernest Hemingway

In Spain the dead are more alive than the dead of any other country in the world.
– Federico Garcia Lorca

Spain is an overflow of sombreness . . . a strong and threatening tide of history meets you at the frontier.
– Wyndham Lewis

WE CROSS THE SPANISH border and don't even notice it. One moment we are passing familiar cobblestone sidewalks and multicolored apartment buildings in the rural edges of Portugal, the next we are greeted by advertisement signs in Spanish and a sea of beige and white houses.

Many people hardly know the difference between Portugal and Spain, oftentimes forgetting that Portugal shares a small slice of the Iberian Peninsula with its close Spanish cousin. But even though the Portuguese and Spanish languages may share roots in Latin, they sound completely different, and, besides the basics, a speaker of one cannot be understood easily by a speaker of the other. The two peoples might share a love of Iberian pork or codfish, but the Portuguese devote much more attention to the sea while the larger farmlands of Spain provide the thinly sliced ham that the Spanish so often serve as appetizers.

Their habits, too, are entirely different. In Portugal, people will take an entire hour off work for lunch (*almoço*), one of the biggest meals of the day besides dinner. But in Spain, everything seems to shut down entirely after lunch, the streets empty save for tourists, as everyone goes indoors for their *siesta*—a phenomenon that does not occur in Portugal, contrary to popular belief. Those in Spain also eat dinner much later. Most restaurants in Spain do not even open until 8pm, and we were surprised at how many families with young children remained at dinner until midnight.

In other words, in the eyes of those who know Portugal or Spain well, these two countries could not be any more different. But the border we cross has not always been there, and these two distinct cultures were once considered one and the same, or else divided up by foreigners very differently than how we do today. When the Romans conquered Hispania, they did not call the people Portuguese and Spanish but Hispanic, and drew borders according to the geography, environment, and the various tribes that occupied the peninsula. Yet borders are not meaningless, and the various divisions drawn throughout ancient Iberia have come to shape its history.

Our first stop in Spain is Mérida, a rather small town not containing many popular tourist sites, except for its most impressive attraction: the ruins of the former Roman city, Augusta Emerita. We enter the city on foot from across the Rio Guadiana and immediately recognize its Roman past. The bridge crossing the river was built by the Romans, and before we even step foot beyond the crumbling city walls, we see a familiar statue greeting our entrance into the city, namely the famous Capitoline Wolf sculpture, with the infant Romulus and Remus suckling the she-wolf. Below the statue, a plaque reads:

LA CIUDAD DE ROMA A LA CIUDAD DE MÉRIDA AYER AUGUSTA EMERITA.
From the city of Rome to the city of Mérida, formerly Augusta Emerita.

This is not the only sign of the city's strong Roman heritage. The mosaics on the streets bear images related to Augusta Emerita. Even our hotel is named *Nova Roma,* and upon checking in, we are amused to see its walls covered with copies of famous busts, sculptures, and pottery discovered from the city's ancient ruins. But what surprises us the most is the city's acceptance and even pride as a former Roman city—yet more than that, as having been founded by the first emperor of Rome, Augustus Caesar.

Indeed, in 25 BC, Augustus founded Augusta Emerita (present-day Mérida) and made it the capital of Lusitania, one of three new provinces that would then divide the Iberian peninsula. Augusta Emerita was founded as a colony for two of Augustus' legions to settle in (*'Emeritus'* in Latin means 'veteran'), as rewards for their service. These legions—called *Legio V Alaudae* and *Legio X Gemina*—had fought in the Cantabrian War, which was the campaign that, in 19 BC, would ultimately complete the Roman conquest of Hispania. The first residents of this colony, therefore, were not indigenous Iberians but Romans—specifically veterans loyal to Caesar Augustus—originating from Italy. Perhaps it should not come as such a surprise that their descendants still show their Roman pride.

Of the 45 towns in Lusitania, only five of these (Augusta Emerita included) were true *Italic*-Roman colonies.

The rest were home to indigenous Iberians, who had lived there since as early as the 4th century BCE. Only Olissippo (modern Lisbon) was granted full Roman citizenship, while three towns (including Évora) received partial citizenship rights. All of the towns had to pay taxes and provide men for the Imperial Roman army. Contrary to the propaganda spread by the Romans in Italy, these indigenous Iberians were not barbarians who needed to be civilized; they had already built countless cities well-connected by roads across the peninsula without the help of the Romans.

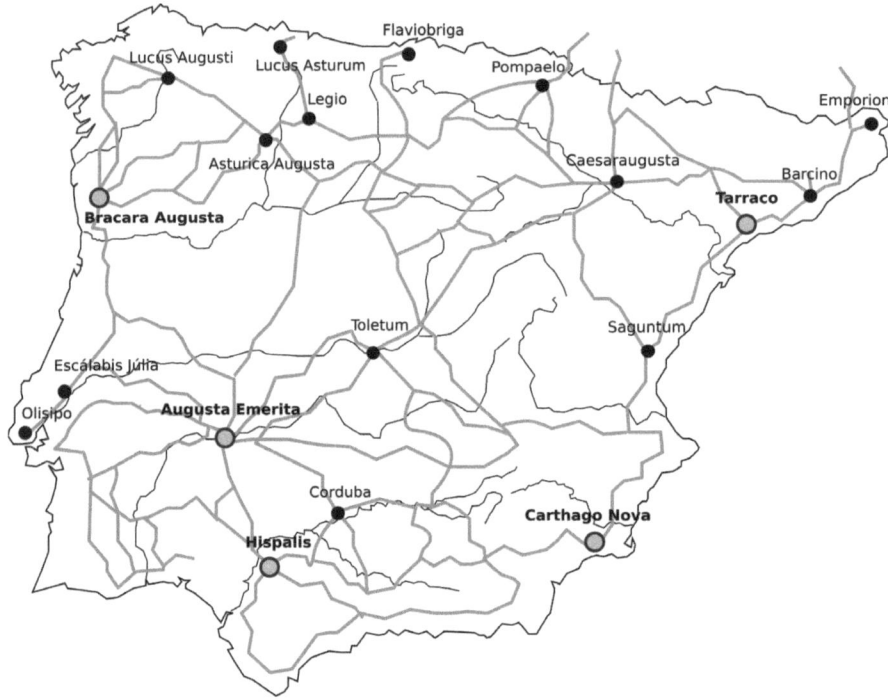

5.1 Map of Roman Hispania

In fact, Augustus chose the strategic location of Augusta Emerita based on its position at an important crossroads of western Iberia. For Augusta Emerita sat at the intersection of two major roads: the north-south Silver Way and the east-west road that connected Olissippo with the Eastern coast of modern Spain. Roads also linked important inland cities with the port cities on the coast, making the movement of goods, people, and armies swift and efficient. Moreover, the site lay nestled in low hills at the confluence of two rivers, where the land was very fertile. By manipulating the natural landscape, moving the river, and building aqueducts, sewage, and terraces, the Romans were able to successfully found their new colony, with forum, temple, amphitheater, and all.

While many monuments of ancient Augusta Emerita can still be seen today, the temple of Diana is one of the most spectacular, and we cannot resist eating dinner at one of the many restaurants bordering its remains. We order Iberian ham, croquettes, codfish, and of course, tinto de verano, a popular summer drink in Spain made with wine and soda. It is one of our best meals yet. Our table faces the temple, still standing tall and imposing in the center of the plaza thanks to the king who once built his palace around it. On the side of the temple's platform are the holes where a plaque displaying a yearly calendar or current news would have been posted.

It is easy to imagine this temple once gracing a traditional Roman forum, a place of social gatherings, business, and other activities all occurring at the same time. Even as we eat, a dance group practices their modern dance performance on the makeshift stage built in front of the temple, tourists pass and enter the temple, and people eat and hang around the square. But while Mérida is now considered a smaller Spanish city known more for its Roman ruins than anything else, in its past the city enjoyed special status as the capital of Lusitania, and its position and role in imperial administration also made it a hub of cultural exchange.

Just like any major city today, there was both immigration to and emigration from Augusta Emerita, both within Hispania and the Roman empire overall, though more people were entering than leaving. Immigrants came from such places on the Iberian peninsula as Conímbriga and Olissippo, and even as far away as Rome, Madauros (present-day Algeria), and Nicomedia (on the shores of the Black Sea in present-day Turkey). Many funerary epitaphs found in Augusta Emerita identify the hometown of the deceased person, demonstrating that foreign-born residents of the city wanted to show off, not hide, their places of origin.

By the late Imperial era, whatever their city's past may have been, at least the elite residents of Augusta Emerita fully conceived of themselves as belonging to the Roman Empire. Nowhere is this more clear than in a mosaic from the House of Mithra, a luxury villa situated outside the city walls in the vast rural countryside. This mosaic covered the floor of the owner's office space attached to the atrium, where he would have welcomed guests and attended to business. The figures in it represent the origin of the Roman universe, with Oceanus (the sea) and Caelum (the sky) bordering the top and bottom, Natura (nature) in the middle, and Oriens (the sunrise) and Ocasus (the sunset) bordering east and west. But the most fascinating figures are Mons (the mountains) holding Nix (snow), representing the snow-capped mountains limiting the Roman Empire, and the rivers Nilus (the Nile) and Euphrates, symbolizing the eastern limits of the empire.

It is hard to say whether this mosaic indicates the sentiments of the entire city, much less the provinces of Hispania, but it does suggest that some people, at least, were proud to identify with the expansion of the Roman Empire. And perhaps it was difficult not to, as Augustus did his best to encourage a positive view of his expansionist agenda, which still survives to this day in Mérida's archaeological sites and signs, which praise Augustus as the divine founder of their city.

Augustus built an amphitheater that seated 25,000 people—a massive space considering the city's estimated population of 8000—suggesting that people flocked from all over the peninsula to watch Roman spectacles and engage with Roman culture. The courtyard behind the famous theater housed a "Sacred Room" decorated with statues of Augustus and his adopted sons Tiberius and Gaius.

5.2 Roman Theater of Mérida

Even the forum of Augusta Emerita displayed the same statues which could be found in the Augustan forum back in Rome. In addition to a statue of Romulus, a statue of Aeneas—claimed as the legendary forefather of the Romans and direct ancestor of Augustus—carrying his father and son out of the wreckage of Troy was known to be in both forums, and is now displayed in the wonderful National Museum of Roman Art in Mérida.

Even though Augusta Emerita was founded as a Roman city, its remoteness from Rome, unique environment, and the strong presence of indigenous Iberians and countless immigrants from all over the Empire make it difficult to pin down who, exactly, these Iberian-Romans were. Did they primarily identify as Romans? Or as Hispanic? Did they speak Latin as they did in Rome, or was the common language already slipping away into a dialect that resembled something closer to the ancestor of Spanish and Portuguese? Did the residents of Augusta Emerita, descended as they were from Italic-Roman veterans, consider their indigenous Iberian neighbors as fellow Romans, or as less-civilized natives—or worse, as barbarians?

Mérida, in this sense, holds an air of mystery to us, its past partially obscured by a history lost and rewritten as the Roman empire expanded and collapsed. And when Iberia was conquered by Muslim forces, then Germanic tribes, and lastly Christianity, its former Roman borders being shaped continually by war and politics into their modern places, it is even more difficult to trace the layers of culture, architecture, language, and religion that have left their mark on the cities of Portugal and Spain. When looking back on their history, therefore, it is hard to say precisely what it means to be Spanish, or what it means to be Portuguese.

Our next stop is the Spanish city of Seville, a calm, three hour train ride from Mérida through vineyards and farmlands. If the history of Mérida feels obscure, the history of Seville feels even more vague, despite the visible remains of Roman, Muslim, and Christian occupation. The Romans believed that the city of Hispalis—as Seville was called in antiquity—was founded by Hercules, who (they say) chased the Phoenician goddess Astarte down the Guadalquivir River until Astarte turned right, founding the quarter of Triana (still so-named today), before Hercules turned left, founding Hispalis. In reality, the site has been occupied by various indigenous Iberian kingdoms since the 8th century BC, near the trading sites of the Phoenicians established in the 6th century BC, and it was captured by the Romans during the Second Punic War.

But we did not really come for the modern city of Seville. A twenty-minute drive from Seville lies the archaeological site of Italica, a veterans' colony like Augusta Emerita but nearly two centuries more ancient than Augustus' settlement. In 206 BC, during the Second Punic War, the Roman general Scipio Africanus founded a colony for his Italic soldiers, from which the name 'Italica' derives. It was located about 7 miles from the older and larger city of Hispalis, which was a very important center of trade and industry for the Romans. Italica, however, was primarily residential. After its foundation, more and more people from Italy migrated to Italica, including the *Gens Ulpia* and *Gens Aelia*—the ancestors of the emperors Trajan and Hadrian, respectively.

Hadrian, in particular, took interest in Italica once he became emperor. He gave it more civic rights as a provincial city and expanded the urban area, adding new buildings and renovating others, suggesting a sense of pride and affection for his hometown and province. The part of the city that visitors today can tour dates to the time of Hadrian; the older part still lies unexcavated under the modern-day town of Santiponce.

The villas of Italica boasted numerous mosaics, with a mosaic of various bird species in the House of the Birds being one of the most charming. And despite the remains of Italica seeming scanty in comparison to the well-preserved multiple-story houses of Pompeii, we feel as though Italica's distance from Rome and the center of imperial politics makes it much easier to imagine daily life in a Roman province, and in the ancient world in general.

5.3 Mosaic in the House of Birds

Of course, our delight in these houses is in part due to the wealth of their owners and their consequent extravagance. As we wander the wide, nicely paved streets from a pleasant, finely-decorated villa to the massive luxury bath complex in 100 degree weather, we can certainly imagine how nice it would be as a Hispanic-Roman elite to cool off in a large, marble-lined pool.

But as centuries passed and various kingdoms and religious groups conquered Spain, Italica remained primarily suburban in comparison to the flourishing urban city of Seville. The Spanish identity of Seville fully emerged in the late 15th century, when conquistadores expanded the Spanish empire and its Christian religion to the "New World." Just like Augusta Emerita had been in the Roman world, now Seville found special privilege and wealth at the crossroads of trade with the Americas. In time, it grew into the modern city we recognize today, with its Roman ruins, Muslim palaces, and Christian cathedrals appearing as a familiar patchwork that we now call—perhaps with a slight lisp—*España*.

As the Iberian leg of our journey comes to an end, we reflect on the fact that we have been able to visit four cities in five days and easily research and snap photos of the sites that interested us. Yet if we have learned anything, it is that the ancient world was full of movement, something we tend to overlook or discount since we can hardly conceive of travel without airplanes and cars. But not only did people move, but goods and culture moved as well, so that even the songs heard in taverns on the streets of Seville might not sound so different from those in Greece or Turkey or Iran.

As outsiders in the city today, we hardly understand the Spanish accent and its rapid pace, but we discover universal hand gestures and sounds that make ordering our new obsession—a café bombón—quite easy (and indeed, we have plans to bring this simple yet miraculous concoction of condensed milk and espresso back to the States). We travel on the same ancient roads that have existed for thousands of years, whether we know it or not. We eat food with centuries of history in the cultural exchange that has been happening in the Mediterranean and beyond since the beginning, no matter what languages were spoken and what borders were drawn. It is a modern world, but the world we know.

On our last night in Seville, we decide to watch a traditional Flamenco performance. The heavy folds of the dancer's dress and her stomping feet seem like an infamous Spanish bull fight, while the tangy notes of the guitar and the singer's pulsating melodies echo their roots in the chants of Jewish synagogues and the songs of the Islamic empire. Even the dancer's face, tensed in a kind of passionate trance, is no less mysterious than a Bacchic ritual dance.

At the bar we ask for a drink. "Tinto de verano, por favor."

We are in Spain, after all.

ROME - PART I

An Image in the Making

His ego nec metas rerum nec tempora pono; imperium sine fine dedi.

For them I set neither spatial nor temporal limits; I have granted them empire without end.
—Vergil, *Aeneid 1.278–79*

So we approach the hopeless sprawling of modern Rome—over the yellow Tiber, past the famous pyramid tomb, skirting the walls of the city, till at last we plunge in, into the well-known station, out of all the chaos.
—D.H. Lawrence, *Sea and Sardinia*

THEY SAY ALL ROADS lead to Rome. Of course, we *fly* from Lisbon to the Eternal City, shortening a twenty-day journey by sea and carriage in the ancient world to a mere three hours by plane. But nonetheless, the feeling of arriving in Rome, of the taxi approaching the Aurelian walls, hurtling down cramped alleys and hectic roundabouts only to suddenly come upon the Colosseum in all its 2000-year-old glory—there is nothing quite like it.

As its namesake suggests, it feels as if Rome has been a city forever. While we were both raised in or near major American cities, there is a vastness, a grandeur, and a history to Rome, to its multi-story apartment buildings as decorated and carved as temples, to the old churches towering over every street, to the even more ancient ruins standing proud in the most unlikely of places, that make Rome an imposing city to visit. But it is perhaps our devotion to the Classical world, to our study of the politics and culture and literature of the ancient Romans, that leaves us breathless as we pass yet another gleaming marble column.

After checking into our hotel, we decide to kill a few hours by walking around the Colosseum and surrounding plaza. It is a bad idea. Our last visit to Rome was the autumn of 2021, when there were never more than a handful of tour groups or families at the Colosseum at any given time—the pandemic was still something of a concern, and it was the off-season for tourism—so imagine our surprise when we arrive there this time and it is surrounded by a sea of people. Fighting our way through the crowds to get a good vantage point for a picture, it is impossible not to feel annoyed by the sheer amount of other tourists around us—we miss the quieter, more vacant Rome that we experienced during our semester at the Centro.

But we realize too that this crowded version of Rome, while new to us, in fact probably allows us to both glimpse and experience a more authentic version of ancient Rome. During a day of gladiatorial shows, the Colosseum would have been something of a zoo, with merchants hawking their wares, children complaining, and pigeons pecking underfoot, not to mention the mobs of spectators crowding into the amphitheater. We likewise have to dodge people trying to sell us sunglasses, parents chasing their children, and birds seeking bits of stray panini.

Our first real activity of the day, however, is not the Colosseum but the Largo di Torre Argentina, an archeological site of four Roman temples in the middle of the city that has—to the surprise and disappointment of one tourist—absolutely nothing to do with the country of Argentina. However, this site has special significance to us, as only a month ago it opened to the public. Whereas two years ago we listened to our professors' lectures while standing in front of the fences overlooking the remains, now the grounds are equipped with elevated walkways, signs, and even a small exhibit of various statues found at the site—most of which have never been exhibited for over a hundred years since their discovery.

We eagerly climb down the stairs to the site and take a look around. These temples, we are quickly reminded, are quite old. Each of the four temples was constructed at a different time in the 3rd and 2nd centuries BC, with the first as early as 290 BC. They were modified and restored in the succeeding centuries, and one of them (Temple A) was converted to a Catholic church in the 9th century.

The deities to whom the Roman temples were originally dedicated is not known certainly, which is why we call them Temples A, B, C, and D. However, the site has been identified as the location of one of the most significant moments in Roman history: the assassination of Julius Caesar. Behind Temples B and C stood the Curia of Pompey—a meetinghouse for the Senate—on whose steps Julius Caesar was stabbed twenty-seven times. According to ancient literary sources, Augustus later walled up the building and forbade anyone from entering it. Only its foundations are visible today.

Despite its infamous association with the murder of Julius Caesar, other tourists are sparse, and Rome feels for a moment as it once did to us. But there is something missing. The last time we were here, the site was actually known as a sanctuary for stray cats. As our professors were attempting to lecture about Temple B's structural phases—peripteral to pseudoperipteral—we had amused ourselves by watching the different cats lounging about the ruins, laughing as one hopped up on the top of a broken Corinthian column, swishing its tail as if it owned the place. Now, however, we do not see a single cat slinking across a temple floor, and if they were not removed for the preservation of the site as we suspect, then they are hiding in much quieter, shadier nooks to avoid the new invasion of tourists.

6.1 Largo di Torre Argentina

This is not the first instance of loss in the modern world for the sake of preserving the past. The darker side of archeology, often overlooked, is the loss that must take place to excavate and preserve these magnificent ruins, such as demolishing entire neighborhoods or ceasing construction of public transportation when ruins are discovered while digging.

As we sit down beside the Theater of Marcellus, which was built in the memory of Augustus' nephew and Octavia's son Marcellus, who died tragically at nineteen years old, we cannot help but wish we could see what it once looked like. Now built into the top floor are apartments, and many of the entrances are barred with iron gates. We gaze up at the small windows and wonder how much it would cost to buy an apartment in the Theater of Marcellus, how the apartments are at once preserving and destroying the past.

6.2 Theater of Marcellus

Like the disappearance of the cat sanctuary, the theater is a reminder that we cannot restore the past without losing something of the present. It is the blessing and the curse of studying history, and until we invent time machines—or find magical, time-traveling stones like in the TV show *Outlander*—we must be content with our imaginations to fill in the gaps.

Throughout the trip we often asked ourselves: "If you could go back in time and see Rome at its height, would you?"

At first, neither of us hesitated. "Of course."

But even in fictional TV shows, there is always a cost to traveling back in time. "Even if you would have to leave your family and friends behind?"

It is a silly question, perhaps, but it reminds us that what we long for is not to live in a time different from our own, but rather to have an understanding of people, of a culture that seems so alien to us and yet not very different at all. We like to feel as if history and time have meaning, and maybe even permanence, so that we fill a kind of existential curiosity when looking at a monument that has stood for so long—longer even than the Colosseum.

In order to shake off the burden of our philosophical musings, we head down to the Jewish Ghetto neighborhood to have a much-needed Hugo spritz (Elderflower liqueur with prosecco: our all-time favorite aperitivo), before we have dinner, both of us ordering cacio e pepe pasta. If there is one thing that we both agree is better today than in ancient Rome, it is the food.

Our night does not end with dinner, however, and so we walk to our final destination for the evening: the Baths of Caracalla. Built in the early third century CE under the emperors Septimius Severus and Caracalla, these were a massive public bath complex covering nearly 62 acres and containing over 100 masterpieces of art such as the Farnese Bull and Farnese Hercules. But we are (shockingly) not here to see the Roman ruins at all. Instead, we have tickets for the 'Roberto Bolle and Friends' ballet performance, a two-hour extravaganza boasting of the biggest ballet stars from around the world and performed in front of the ancient ruins.

We find our seats with surprising ease and order. But the moment the lights dim and the dancers come on stage, everyone stands up at once and scrambles to sit in any of the empty front-row seats. We are some of the few stunned tourists who hang back in our assigned seats and crane our necks over the chaos in the crowd—an Italian cultural phenomenon, we suspect—to watch as the dancers begin a beautiful, intimate duet.

The performance is a mix of traditional and modern dance, with our own preference (unsurprisingly) for the more traditional pieces. But we are nonetheless entertained and mesmerized as one dancer leaps into the air for what feels like a minute straight and the other twirls without stopping and the audience can only gasp and applaud. As Classicists, we cannot help but think that this is what the Romans must have felt witnessing gladiators fight or female dancers perform artistic feats in the water, watching as humans do what seems nearly divine. Yet the beautiful thing about dance and performance is that there is no recreating that feeling you get when the music crescendos and the dancer is lifted to impossible heights. All that exists is that moment.

We hardly have time to process the performance and its more eccentric features as we bus home and go to bed, preparing for our first full day in Rome and a lot of walking. We wake up bright and early to visit the Intercollegiate Center for Classical Studies—aka the 'Centro'—where we studied abroad together. Returning to our former neighborhood of Monteverde feels like coming home. Even after nearly two years, the same restaurants, businesses, and cafes line the streets just as we remember them, and the sights, sounds, and smells hit our senses in a familiar symphony. But once we arrive at the Centro, devoid of the professors and students we knew so well there, we are reminded that the word 'history' does not refer only to things that happened 2000 years ago. After a mere two years, the Centro already feels to us like a relic of the past, and we walk around the classrooms and library as if it were another museum, pointing at places we used to sit and work on our Latin and Greek, or objects and books that once had a place in our daily lives.

6.3 Facade of the church in front of the Centro building

All too soon it is time to leave, and we say our goodbyes to Franco and Pina, the Centro's directors. As is the Centro way, from there we go straight to the Vatican for a full day of museum tours. The Vatican Museums are mobbed, which surprises us less than the Colosseum did given its contemporary religious significance, but the sheer mass of people choking each hallway is a sight to behold. Yet after walking through the Egyptian and Roman exhibits, we hike up the last staircase to the Gregorian Etruscan Museum, which is all but empty. Besides one other family perusing the cases of bucchero pottery, it seems we are the only people in the entire Vatican City to have planned a visit to this section.

While we appreciate that it offers us the opportunity for personal space, we are also a little saddened by the lack of interest in Etruscan history demonstrated by the visitors and tour guides. The Egyptian and Roman sections of the Vatican are always crowded—is no one interested in the people who ruled Italy before the Romans? But we suppose that is the way with history. As the saying goes, it is written by the conquerors, and even though the Etruscans had wealth and culture of their own, it was washed away in the power and ideology of Rome.

Even now, the images which shape our idea of Rome today began long ago, such as with the hut of Romulus, mythical founder of Rome, which was preserved for thousands of years on the Palatine (only the post-holes of the hut remain today, but they are still an important display in the archaeological site). Images like the Vatican, Colosseum, and Pantheon align with our idea of Rome much more than the previous Etruscan settlers do. And even Egypt, with its obelisks and half-beast hybrid gods, fits in better with the Roman landscape, still perpetuated by Augustus' defeat of Cleopatra and his lingering imperial propaganda, which finds its mirror in the Catholic Church's missionary traditions.

It seems, in this way, that the past clings to us as much as we cling to the past. With its legends and histories, its monuments and gods, it demands to be remembered as much as we wish to be remembered by those who will come after us.

After several hours of trekking through the Vatican and quickly passing through the Sistine Chapel ("Oh, *that's* the famous hand painting? It's kind of small..."), we take a rest at our hotel only to bus all the way back to Monteverde across the Tiber and have dinner at Lumie di Sicilia, one of our favorite restaurants when we were at at the Centro. This is the only night we can pencil it in, and we cannot resist the call of nostalgia.

The owner does not recognize us as we do him, but it doesn't matter. We order our favorite dishes, a little wine, and for a moment, it feels like no time has passed at all. That is the image of *our* Rome, and it will stay with us even when everything else changes.

6.4 (Above) Post-holes of the hut of Romulus, (below) reconstructed miniature of Palatine Hill

ROME - PART II

A New Light

One begins to realise how old the real Italy is, how man-gripped and how withered...Here since endless centuries man has tamed the impossible mountain side into terraces, he has quarried the rock, he has fed his sheep among the thin woods, he has cut his boughs and burnt his charcoal, he has been half domesticated even among the wildest fastnesses...Life is so primitive, so pagan, so strangely heathen and half-savage. And yet it is human life. And the wildest country is half humanised, half brought under. It is all conscious. Wherever one is in Italy, either one is conscious of the present, or of the mediæval influences, or of the far, mysterious gods of the early Mediterranean. Wherever one is, the place has its conscious genus. Man has lived there and brought forth his consciousness there and in some way brought that place to consciousness, given it its expression, and, really, finished it. The expression may be Proserpine, or Pan, or even the strange "shrouded gods" of the Etruscans or the Sikels, none the less it is an expression. The land has been humanised, through and through: and we in our own tissued consciousness bear the results of this humanisation. So that for us to go to Italy and to penetrate into Italy is like a most fascinating act of self-discovery—back, back down the old ways of time. Strange and wonderful chords awake in us, and vibrate again after many hundreds of years of complete forgetfulness.
—D.H. Lawrence, Sea and Sardinia

As our five days in Rome continue in full swing, the city's hostile summer environment catches up to us. Mosquitos linger at every corner, threatening to bite even the smallest bit of skin left unprotected. The humidity is unbearable as temperatures reach new heights, culminating in an outrageous 108°F on our last day in Rome. The tourist crowds only grow more dense, and our stamina after waking up early and walking all day in the hot sun wanes until we cannot help but look forward to leaving the city.

However, we still have many sights to see, with the first being Ostia Antica. Near the modern coastal city of Ostia, only an hour outside of Rome by public transit, this is one of our most beloved archeological sites from our time at the Centro. On the train we spot umbrellas, towels, and groups of teenagers ready to go to the beach—a pitstop we also plan to make after our time at the site.

Having seen how crowded the Colosseum and Vatican Museums were, we expect that the archaeological site of Ostia Antica will be packed as well. But to our surprise, the site is more or less empty, and the sounds of nature—insects chattering, leaves rustling—rather than the din of tourists fill our ears as we walk down the road leading to the ancient city gate. In fact, unlike the last time we were here during autumn, a lush spring had caused the wild grasses to grow taller than the ruins themselves in some places, so that it feels as if the site has been abandoned, belonging not to us but to nature.

7.1 Ancient Roman road leading into Ostia Antica

The city would not have felt like this in ancient Roman times: originally a military camp situated on the river Tiber, Ostia developed into one of the most important commercial centers and port cities for Rome, with an estimated population of 100,000 at its height. Not only that, Ostia was an international city, and visible in the mosaics decorating the marketplace are names of cities that the business owners originated from, such as the African cities of Carthage and Gumma and the Sardinian city of Caralis. Ostia's state of preservation, furthermore, is comparable to that of Pompeii. Fragmentary mosaics, marble floors, and frescoes still adorn the buildings, and many of the structures even now boast their original roofs and second floors. Compared to the meager foundations that comprise most archaeological sites, Ostia Antica is a Classicist's dream.

And it is for this reason that we audaciously plan to explore the entire city (at least, the third of it that has yet been excavated). After walking for about two hours straight on dirt paths and overgrown fields, the sun beating down on us with little shade, we quickly realize that this is not feasible. Each street and alleyway leads us to ever more surprising structures, beautiful frescoes, and enchanting mosaics. Large, two story buildings with vaulted hallways, fully equipped with baths and gardens and peristyle courtyards, leave us breathless. We have hardly seen a fifth of what we wanted to when it is time for lunch, and soon, the beach.

Despite our failed attempt at seeing every house and street in Ostia Antica, we do learn a lot from what we do—and do not—see. If Ostia Antica, the smaller port city, was *this* sprawling, *this* grand, *this* developed, then Rome must have been even bigger. It is a sobering realization, and as we pass by house after house, market after market, the theater, several temples, fountains, baths, apartments, parks, and so on, we easily fill in the realities of city life that we have been experiencing all week—the crowds, the smell, the heat, the noise, and the sheer movement of businesses, markets, and day-to-day life. While the Colosseum and the Pantheon are meant to awe us by their grandeur, what really shocks us, at least, is how ultimately familiar the environment feels when we step away from the propaganda of Imperial Rome.

Yet the site is no longer a city, and at some point after the decline of Rome, Ostia Antica was indeed abandoned. Nature has long since asserted her dominion over the land, filling empty rooms and houses with tall, prickly weeds and formidable bushes and grass into which we did not dare venture too far. The tall pine trees drip sticky sap over the stone roads, lizards slither along foundation walls, beetles and ants trudge their own paths through the dirt, and butterflies and bees waft from flower to flower. Not enough tourists walk around the site to form natural pathways further away from the main roads, and we find ourselves growing tired of picking our way around gnarled, spiky plants and families of beetles. In the end, we are only visitors, and it is time to leave.

We take public transit to the beachfront and pay for two chairs under an umbrella. The beach is packed, with Italian families and tourists crowding the warm Mediterranean water. We sink under the calm, rolling waves in relief, glad to just relax. The warm water, the hot sun, the slight breeze—it's hard to imagine anything better.

"Wait, did the Romans go to the beach?" we ask ourselves.

After a few minutes debating the likelihood of Roman beachgoers and giving up to float in the water, we head back to our chairs to read for a bit before beginning the trek home, where we still have more to see.

For dinner and drinks, we head to Piazza Navona. This piazza stands on the site of the ancient Stadium of Domitian, inaugurated by the emperor in 86 AD. The shape of the stadium, a long and narrow rectangle that is curved at one end, has influenced the current layout of Piazza Navona. Domitian intended for athletic competitions to take place in his stadium, a far cry from the restaurants, merchants, and tourists that now fill the square. But it is nonetheless still a site of spectacle, which we understand well as a musician sets up

7.2 Bath complex in Ostia Antica

his microphone and speaker right in front of our table. This Piazza suffered a very different fate from the abandonment of Ostia Antica, and we cannot help but wonder how the stadium had been used throughout the centuries so that it kept its original shape. What keeps places from being abandoned? Which site has been better "preserved," so to speak—Ostia Antica and her static, excavated ruins of bare structures and roads or the Stadium of Domitian whose functions may have changed but whose spacious, public arena is still used and lived in by modern Romans?

Our last stop for the night is the famous gelato shop, Giolitti, before walking to the Pantheon. It seems everyone else has the same idea. We fight the large swathes of tourists and merchants selling light-up toys and flowers to take a picture of the temple-turned-church. But the crowds are to be expected, and for good reason. The Pantheon is an intimidating building, its columns intact and towering before us, the large dome behind it only adding to its air of mystery and prestige. It does not matter if the people snapping photos in front of it do not know who Marcus Agrippa was or even the Emperor Hadrian. The legacy of the monument as an image of Rome has roots as deep as its foundation.

The famous inscription reading 'M. AGRIPPA' on the front of the Pantheon only tells part of the truth. Marcus Agrippa had built a temple on the same site, but it was destroyed by fire. The Pantheon that stands today was constructed by Hadrian ca. 125 CE, but he decided to leave the name of the original building's architect on the front. Even as a foreigner hailing from the province of Hispania, Hadrian understood the power of the Pantheon as an image of Rome. The Romans of Hadrian's time would read 'M. AGRIPPA' and be reminded of the great man who had contributed to the construction of Augustus' imperial power a century before, and consequently the power which Hadrian held; now tourists of the twenty-first century see the Pantheon and stand in awe of the architectural prowess of the ancient people. In both cases, it is not necessarily the truth behind the monument that matters but the feeling that the monument provokes. In this way, Hadrian's rebuilding was a creative act of *imagining* Rome, not unlike what we do today.

In fact, it is interesting that many of the most iconic images of Rome today were actually built by emperors who did not hail from Rome or even Italy: Hadrian, who built the Pantheon, and Trajan, who built a forum, markets, and massive column, were both born in Italica, near the modern city of Seville in Spain. What does it mean to call these monuments 'Roman'? Though popular culture today tends to treat the ancient city of Rome as a cultural monolith, characterized by gladiators fighting in the Colosseum and toga-clad statues decorating the forum, in ancient times it would have been much more diverse, in communication with its provinces. 'Rome' as we know it was built physically on seven hills, but its development as a city and culture is actually indebted to its wide-ranging empire.

Even all the marble and statues and pottery that we admire were imported from as far abroad as modern-day Egypt, Portugal, and Iran. Hadrian himself, though from the provinces, prided himself on collecting artifacts and art from all over the world—especially Egypt—and displaying them in his luxurious villa in Tivoli. These statues now grace the Egyptian and Roman exhibits at the Vatican, and in this way, they also speak to the cultural (and historically political) dominion which the Catholic Church inherited from the Roman Empire.

Propaganda, which nowadays we might think of merely as posters and ads, also plays a huge role in art, literature, and architecture. While the Egyptian statues in Hadrian's villa, or foundational literature such as Virgil's *Aeneid*, or iconic monuments such as the Pantheon all serve artistic and cultural purposes, they also promote (and arguably subvert) the message of an expanding, powerful empire. As is seen by Hadrian's rebuilding of the Pantheon and our visit to Mérida, founded by Augustus and still advertised that way, it is clear that Roman propaganda reached—and still does reach—very far and wide.

We feel these influences during our tour of the Palatine Hill, and especially of the House of Augustus. A section of the supposed house of the first Roman emperor, now enclosed in a large black building, had not been available the last time we were here. We enter through thick curtains that darken the inside so that a video can be projected on the wall. The video gives a rundown of the layout of the house, how Augustus came to buy the property, how the second floor still has his beloved office he liked to call 'Syracuse,' and even mentions his plans to renovate. It all sounds very convincing, despite the fact that there is no positive evidence that this was Augustus' residence. The only evidence we have to suggest that is its location next to the ruins of the temple of Apollo, where ancient sources tell us that Augustus made his home. This shaky proof, however, does not hinder the museum organizers from putting on a full exhibit about the House of Augustus without a hint of doubt, and at the end of the tour, even we are half-convinced. After all, it is always more enjoyable to believe the story told, whether it is true or not.

Another exhibit we see later that day in the museum in Trajan's Markets also centers on Augustus. But this time, it is about two statue heads of Augustus—one depicting him younger, the other older—that were recently discovered and restored. At the end of a long hallway of artifacts, we sit down and look at the two statue heads which have been placed side-by-side in the middle of a circular room. Then a light shines on the younger head, and an audio begins. It is a conversation in English between a younger Augustus (in a thick Italian accent) who holds lofty ideals of a unified, peaceful republic and an older, more cynical Augustus (also with an Italian accent). We cannot help but laugh at the snarky comments made about Livia and the naiveté assigned to the younger Augustus. Even today, it seems, we continue to grapple with Augustus' rise to power and his reign, and his obscure persona, both young and old, still remains a question for us to answer, which was to a certain extent exactly how Augustus wished it to be.

The next day we take a network of buses to visit another ancient site about an hour and a half outside of Rome. The city of Praeneste (modern-day Palestrina) was a powerful and prominent Latin city that became allied with Rome in the fourth century BC. But in the first century BC, the general Sulla turned it into a veteran's colony, and subsequently many Roman elites, including Augustus, decided to construct villas there (no less because of its magnificent valley views). It also had a massive temple of the goddess Fortuna Primigenia, which was constructed on top of a high hill, and which is the main reason why we have come to the city.

The bus drops us off at the bottom of the slope, and we stare up at the temple. Even before reaching the stairs and ramps that we must mount to enter the complex, we have to journey up through the modern-day town of Palestrina. Ascending a seemingly endless set of stairs that winds past apartments and quiet cafés, we feel as we imagine the ancient pilgrims to the site did as they approached the temple of Fortuna: a bit tired, a bit sweaty, and hopeful that what we will find at the top is worth the trek.

But we have not come to consult the oracle or offer a votive to the goddess. We are here instead because of a famous mosaic depicting the Nile that is housed in the museum. The river snakes up the mosaic, flooding the lands which are crowded with Romans of the Egyptian city of Alexandria and even Ethiopians at the imagined border of Egypt, as well as a delightful range of animals like rhinos and lions and crocodiles, all labeled in Greek. The mosaic is a perfect symbol of the Eastern influences seen in Palestrina's ancient history. Even in the 7th century BC, before it was a Roman town, Praeneste traded with the Phoenicians. Commercial contact with the Eastern world continued throughout the Roman period, but perhaps the best example of the role of the East in Praeneste is the calendar.

Prior to the first century BC, the Roman calendar was rather disorganized, having no fixed length (the city's priests, elected annually, decided when the year should end). The months were, at least in theory, aligned with the lunar cycle, and the Romans believed that there was a strong connection between the course of the moon and the course of the year. But in 45 BC, Julius Caesar enacted a significant program of reforms to the calendar to standardize it. He set the length of the year at 365 days with a leap-day added every four years—which we still observe today—in order to align the length of the year with the cycle of the sun. The calculations of the solar cycle came from the work of Egyptian astronomers, and in fact, Julius Caesar supposedly learned about them while at a dinner party in Alexandria with Cleopatra. The Alexandrian astronomer Sosigenes returned to Rome with Caesar and aided in establishing the new Roman calendar.

The Roman calendar, comprised as it was of religious festivals and anniversaries of important historical events, was deeply tied with the Romans' cultural identity. For this reason, it was a valuable tool for Augustus to use as he aimed to strengthen his position as emperor. By linking himself closely with the calendar, he could link himself closely with the Roman identity itself. Moreover, the fact that the year now matched the solar cycle aligned with his propaganda of associating himself with the sun and Apollo, and the usurpation of Egyptian knowledge for the Roman calendar paralleled his defeat of Antony and Cleopatra at Actium. And it is Praeneste where Augustus decided to set up a massive calendar inscribed in stone (called *fasti* in Latin), testifying both to the importance of the city in the Roman world and to its inherent nature as a point of contact between Rome and the East. Augustus' choice to put the calendar in Praeneste emphasizes that he is not merely the ruler of the city of Rome but commands her extensive empire as well.

Despite its significance in antiquity, however, Palestrina is hardly visited today by tourists. We are the only people hiking up the stairs on the way up to the museum besides the rare locals or cats—both of whom stare at us in quiet reproach for the intrusion—and we are the only visitors in the entire museum. Once again, it

7.3 View from the Temple of Fortuna in Palestrina

seems that even powerful sites in the ancient world have been swept away by the Imperial regime, even though Augustus knew full well its worth at the time and used the city's history to strengthen his own legitimacy.

After bussing back to Rome, we stop for a brief lunch before our visit to the Capitoline Museum. We are exhausted from our travels, but we have already bought the tickets so we decide to visit a few of our favorite statues and artifacts and call it a day. Little did we know, however, that this visit would utterly change our perspective on the ancient world. After endless rooms and statues, hidden at the end of a barely-visible hall-way, we come across a temporary exhibit about lamps in Pompeii. The walls are painted a suspiciously bright yellow, but we enter anyways and are soon blown away.

It turns out that, in the several years of studying the Classical world, the importance of lamps had never really occurred to us. This may sound silly and an obvious fact of life before electricity, but for us, having visited countless roofless villas, houses, and rooms, as well as having seen hundreds of mosaics and frescoes under bright fluorescent lights, this realization is, in fact, monumental. For instance, the brightly colored walls of Roman houses and villas were painted in ruby-reds and yellows and blacks—though garish to us today—because these colors appear better in candlelight. For half or more of the day, these intricate mosaics and walls, adorned with paintings of mythological scenes which are now analyzed in detail by Classicists, would have been shrouded in darkness or covered in shade, only illuminated by fire which mostly gave off light sideways.

Besides the implications for how a Roman villa or house would look and feel at certain times of the day and year, this exhibit gives us a better understanding of why elite Romans were so concerned with the layout of their villas (as attested in the many letters they wrote about their properties). It is like the modern concern for an open-floor-plan on HGTV except entirely centered on light, the heat of the sun, and shade rather than the unobstructed sightline from kitchen to living room. Some villas were built so that most of the house was shaded at the hottest part of the day, but at dawn and evening, light could still come in through the windows. Rooms meant for use in the winter were mostly painted black to hide smoke stains from candles, which would be burned more often. Summer rooms, on the other hand, were constructed underground to take advantage of the soil's natural coolness (a lack of air-conditioning, it seems, is a timeless problem).

But the most fascinating part of this exhibit is about the lamps and candelabras themselves. Although we have seen innumerable lamps in every archeological museum we have gone to, we would merely admire some of the interesting or funny figures placed on the top of the lamps and move on. Now, we realize that the light shining from the lamp would cast shadows on the walls depending on what figure was placed above it. One of the most compelling was the figure of a bat, which, when lit, cast a shadow of three bats on the wall—a terrifying but charming reference to a mythological story of the Minyades, the three daughters of King Min-yas, who got turned into bats because they resisted worshiping Dionysus.

Candelabras, on the other hand, which were typically fashioned tall, thin, and often florally decorated, would hold aloft candles around the house. But the most luxurious candelabras were sculpted as people, meant to mimic the slaves who would hold lamps for their owners, a bronze hand outstretched in eternal service. These lamps would be the silent watchers in all parts of the house, even in the bedroom, a motif often used in literature when describing intimate scenes between lovers.

In our first-ever virtual reality experience offered within the exhibit, we are able to light several candles around a *triclinium* and see the effects the light had not only on the mosaic and wall frescoes, but the very ambience of the space as a whole. As the golden light of the candle casts the virtual red and black walls in a sultry glow, reflected on the bronze of the standing candelabra, we can easily imagine how compelling those late-night dinner parties, or *convivia*, would have been—not unlike Greek symposiums—and how easily conversation could slip into the philosphical or even intimate.

This exhibit and our new realizations follow us the next day when we go to the Palazzo Massimo, possibly our favorite museum of all time and the last one we will visit in Rome on this trip. We both had our Centro site reports here (Zoë's on the bronze Boxer statue and Grace's on Livia's garden frescoes) and one of our first escapades together was a trip to the museum to prepare for the assignment, so the museum holds a sentimental as well as intellectual place in our lives.

As we look around the room containing the garden frescoes that we know all too well, decorated with elaborate shrubbery and birds, we now cannot help but wonder how the room would be lit. We imagine candelabras in the shape of trees, lit at the ends of multiple branches, scattered about the room, casting shadows of larger-than-life trees. This frescoed room was originally underground in the imperial villa at Prima Porta, and in the thick of the summer heat in Rome (which we are now well acquainted with), we know it must have provided a cool, enchanting retreat, and like a true garden, mingled both shadow and light.

As our time in Rome draws near its end, our "discovery" of lamps and their significance in the ancient world gains new meaning. It is not only interesting for us as Classicists, but important as a reminder that, even when we think we understand antiquity, there is still room for surprises and revelations. Although history is too often now buried or destroyed, we can and should still look for new angles and shed new light not only on the past but also the people who lived it. After all, it is the lives of those people and the lessons they learned which we strive to understand, from the stories they told to the candles they lit, and in this way, hope to illuminate our own lives.

On our last night in Rome, we squeeze our way past the crowds to the edge of the Trevi Fountain. We close our eyes, throw the coins over our left shoulders, and smile. It's a good omen: *We will be back.*

7.4 Two walls from Livia's frescoes

THE BAY OF NAPLES

Unearthing Treasures & Tragedies

How am I to describe the coast of Campania, a fertile region so blessed with pleasant scenery that it was manifestly the work of Nature in a happy mood? Campania has a wealth of different kinds of forest, breezes from many mountains, an abundance of wheat, vines and olives, splendid fleeces produced by its sheep, fine-necked bulls, numerous lakes, rich sources of rivers and springs that flow over the whole region. Its many seas and harbours and the bosom of its lands are open to commerce, while even the land eagerly runs out into the sea as if to assist mankind.
– Pliny the Elder, *Natural History 3.40–41.*

As our train departs from Rome's Termini station and makes for the coastal town of Baiae, we imagine we are elite Romans on our way to luxurious villas on the Bay of Naples. It would not be far from what actually took place in ancient Rome. As the summer heat intensified and the city became unbearable, the wealthy would escape the humidity and mosquitos and sweaty crowds for the cooler climate down south, where their villas sprawled and opened to the ocean breeze. And after five days in Rome, we too feel the call of Campania.

Indeed, starting in the first century BCE, Roman elites transformed Baiae from a humble port town into a spot for luxury beachfront villas, something akin to the Hamptons outside New York City. Many wealthy individuals, like Balbus, the manager of Caesar's business affairs, as well as such notable names as Julius Caesar, Cicero, Mark Antony, and Nero, had villas there. Baiae was notorious in Roman society for being a location of vice, sexual licentiousness, and immoral excess.

We arrive at our hotel in Baiae in the afternoon and immediately make our way to the Parco Archeologico delle Terme di Baia ('Archaeological Site of the Baths of Baiae'), which is somewhat of a misnomer since the site actually contains the remains of a villa and two temples (to Mercury and to Venus) in addition to three different bath complexes. The view is stunning, and we have no trouble understanding why the owner chose to build his villa on a slope overlooking the bay.

The villa's several terraces boast of all the comforts and luxuries of Roman life, and countless rooms where guests would have stayed suggest the infamous parties that they surely had, some even on their yachts. The baths and temples are no less impressive, with expansive rooms once dripping in marble and domed ceilings that remind us of the Pantheon. Though by now we have visited more ruins of baths and villas than we can count, these are perhaps the ones that most truly embody the sense of luxury that the ancient Romans loved.

Later that night, we have dinner at one of the nearby restaurants on the strip along the marina. It is a fight to get seated: the restaurant owner claims that all the tables have been booked, but after consulting with his wife in rapid-fire Italian, he changes his mind and decides he can squeeze us in the busy timetable.

Despite our skepticism at his anxiety—it is already 9pm and the restaurant is still empty—sure enough several large Italian families, some bringing more than four generations with them, dressed in elegant clothes and fine jewelry, begin to arrive. They seem to know the restaurant owner and even the other families, as if they frequent this spot every summer and are now old friends. We feel out of place in our sneakers and damp hair from our showers, and the thought occurs to us that perhaps Baiae is still very much a summer retreat for wealthy Italians today, just as it has always been.

As if on cue, a family of cats appears among the tables where we are sitting outside, hoping to beg for scraps. The mother makes a whole show of breastfeeding her three adorable kittens as the father stands watch, waiting for the first restaurant-goer to crack at the adorable domestic scene. It won't be us, we think, as we finish off the last piece of our 4-euro-priced bread basket. We eat our dinner quickly and leave, glad to escape the clatter of screaming children and berating mothers, as well as the critical glances sent our way. Besides, we have a very, very big day tomorrow, and it is the main reason we have come to Baiae: the *Parco Archeologico Sommerso di Baia*, otherwise known as the Submerged Archaeological Site of Baiae.

The next morning, we take a bus up a steep, winding road to the Castello di Baia, an 18th-century palace constructed by the Spanish viceroy of Naples, which houses the archaeological museum. With their collection of artifacts from archaic to Roman times, we hope to distract ourselves from the anxiety we feel over the fact that we are scheduled to go scuba diving later that afternoon.

In spite of our preoccupying thoughts, the museum manages to captivate us. It tells a story of the Bay of Naples from its earliest times, displaying objects like a lekythos (a type of narrow vase) from the seventh century BC with an inscription in the Euboean alphabet. We see the artifacts from each period in chronological order as we walk from room to room, thus getting a clear picture of how daily life in Baiae and the nearby cities of Cumae and Puteoli developed.

One of our favorite exhibits is a recreation of a cave from Egypt that was located along the trade route between India and Rome. Its connection to the Bay of Naples is not immediately obvious until we see that there is an inscription from the year 4 BC carved into the inner wall of the cave. It was written by a slave named Laudanes from Puteoli, a city near Baiae. Soon we see a second carving from another Puteolan slave of the first century AD named Lysas. By this trade route, goods such as perfumes, spices, and fine objects came from India into the hands of the Roman elite, and the two inscriptions add nuance to our understanding of just how lavish life in Roman Baiae must have been. Not only did they live in sprawling, mansion-like villas, but on a day-to-day basis they had access to things like exotic spices and jewelry from the East, which even today we consider luxury goods.

8.1 View on the road up to the Castello di Baia

After leaving the museum, we try to eat lunch despite the butterflies in our stomachs: we have nothing else planned before our next activity, and it is hard to think of anything but what we are about to do. We arrive at the scuba diving center fifteen minutes early, only to quickly learn that Italian time still very much functions in Baiae, and we are introduced to our diving guides, Alexander and Carlo, with all the unhurried charm of resort hosts. Alexander and Carlo can tell we are nervous and immediately joke about it until we cannot help but relax too. We are fitted in our fins, suits, and goggles, and given a rundown of our diving equipment as well as emergency procedures. Finally, we think, they are going to start the dive, and a swoop of nerves hits us. But no. First, they bring us to another room where we are given a presentation on the archeological history of the site.

The fact that many of Baiae's ruins are now underwater, it turns out, is due to the phenomenon of brady-seism, which refers to the gradual raising or lowering of the earth's surface caused by changes in the amount of magma underneath volcanoes. The entire area of the Phlegrean Fields (the volcanic site on which both Baiae and Puteoli lie) was sinking during the time that the ancient Romans occupied the site, but because the rate was so slow—mere centimeters per year—the bradyseism had no impact for centuries. Earthquakes and disease led to the abandonment of Baiae in the 3rd century CE, but not until the 5th century did the town become so submerged that it was impossible to inhabit. The ground is now rising, and our presenter joked that soon enough the ruins would once again be above water—and that they would be out of a job.

For now, underwater archeological work in the 20th century uncovered mosaics, statuary, artifacts, and the remains of buildings dating to the Roman imperial period. When we heard that this archaeological site was open to the public, we could not resist the opportunity: never before had we gone *underwater* to see Roman ruins, and when or where else would we get to do so?

But it is still scuba diving, something that neither of us had ever done before and that terrifies us both. After the presentation finishes, we all walk out to the dock and board our boat. The captain of the boat smokes a cigar as he steers us out of the marina—undeniably cool—and ties up our boat to a buoy. We nervously slip on our fins and goggles. Carlo will be our personal diving guide, while Alexander will guide another couple joining our excursion. Despite his age, Carlo elegantly forward-somersaults into the ocean—also undeniably cool—in full diving gear, and everyone laughs at our shocked faces. Grace jumps into the water first, where Carlo practices a few emergency procedures with her. Zoë is next, and once we have both proven that we can empty our goggles of water and reinsert our oxygen mouthpieces while underwater, we are good to go. Carlo looks at us carefully, sensing our nerves.

"You okay, girls?" he asks.

We nod, even though Zoë can hardly respond. Carlo doesn't speak a lot of English, but somehow we under-stand each other perfectly.

He smiles. "If you are scared, just hold my hand."

This turns out to be exactly what happens. We descend down without incident, equalizing the pressure in our ears as we go. Even though the depth is hardly more than fifteen feet, the seabed is filled with sand and rock, and we try to get used to breathing only with our mouths as Carlo guides us—sure enough, holding our hands—to the archeological site.

Once we get situated, the ocean feels very calm. Fish of all shapes and colors glide past without heeding us at all, and the water is warm and begins to clear as we move away from the buoy. Thankfully, Carlo continues to take us arm in arm, one of us on each side. He leads us slowly to the first mosaic, which depicts a black and white illustration of two athletes, most likely wrestlers or boxers. We are in awe as we slowly descend and hover over the mosaic, passing our hands along the stone and tracing the figures. It is rare to be able to touch mosaics, and to see it from above as fish gently nibble on the sand in between the small stones is like entering into another world, not wholly the past but also not quite the present.

But as we swim on, we pass an underwater plaque containing a map showing the villa's ground plan, and we are reminded that this is an archeological site. The site is called the Villa of the Prothyrum, a Roman luxury villa so called because it has unique remains of a marble entryway (*prothyrum* in Latin). In addition to the mosaic of athletes and the entryway, we see other black-and-white geometric mosaics as well as parts of the villa's private bath complex. We also swim over the ancient road in front of the villa and see the foundational walls and thresholds of shops that once lined the front of the property.

8.2 Underwater mosaic of boxers

Besides seeing the structures from this new perspective, what excites us most is when Carlo hands us fragments of pottery. They look at once familiar and foreign: the clay bodies and handles of vases are the same shapes and sizes as ones we have seen in museum display cases, but having been underwater for centuries, they are covered in multicolored barnacles and other soft, mossy marine life. Holding these ancient objects in our hands, we marvel at the fact that we are experiencing them in a way that no Roman could have ever imagined.

Then it is time for the second location, the Nymphaeum of Claudius. We are better prepared after our first round of diving for the descent, and we slip down the metal chain with ease. This site was part of the imperial villa of the emperor Claudius. Niches set in the walls of the rectangular room contain several statues of the imperial family and two of the god Dionysus. An apse at the end of the room holds statues of Odysseus and his helmsman Baios—who is actually the mythological namesake of Baiae—as they serve unmixed wine to sedate the cyclops Polyphemus.

The original statues have been removed from the water and now live in the archaeological museum in order to protect them from further water damage, but replicas have been placed underwater in the spots where they were found. We swim around them carefully, amazed that the original statues survived two millennia in the sea.

8.3 Ancient ruins of a luxurious villa in Baiae overlooking the Bay of Naples

The Nymphaeum was a space sacred to the nymphs, female divinities of nature, and would have been decorated so as to look like the interior of a cave. It is interesting to think that it was supposed to *resemble* a natural space, offering Claudius and his guests the opportunity to feel like they were in the wilderness while in fact lounging in luxury, but now has actually *become* one. Ancient Romans loved to simulate nature and create cultivated outdoor spaces, especially at their villas, and it strikes us as somewhat ironic and even fitting that the Nymphaeum now belongs to the sea and its marine residents.

As we drive back to the marina on the boat, our driver once again pulls out a cigar, and even Carlo lights a cigarette. We park in the marina and head back to the diving center to shower and change, still reeling from the dives. It was enchanting, perilous, and thought-provoking at the same time, and we have a hard time pinpointing exactly what it was that made the experience so poignant and powerful.

We have dinner almost immediately after even though it is only 7pm (a very early dinnertime in Europe). Diving, it turns out, is an extremely physical activity. The restaurant overlooks the bay as the sun sets in a picturesque view, yet we are the only people there. By the time we get back to the hotel, we are exhausted, and soon fall fast asleep.

In the morning, we travel to Naples, passing Pozzuoli (the modern name of Puteoli) and the remains of a marketplace and amphitheater—the third largest in Italy—on the way. But our main destination for the day is the National Archaeological Museum of Naples, which we had visited with the Centro in autumn of 2021. At the time, Naples had been a bit chilly, and in photos we were even wearing sweaters. Now the city could not be more humid, and we half-miss the sea breezes of Baiae. Even worse, the museum is not air conditioned.

Our first stop is the special exhibit called *Magna Graecia* (Latin for 'Great Greece'), which was the ancient Romans' term for the coastal regions of southern Italy. It costs us an extra euro to enter, but it is more than worth the price. After slipping on the mandatory shoe protectors, we immediately step onto 2000-year-old marble and mosaic floors from Pompeii, which have been restored and moved for this exhibit. We are amazed to be walking on colored marble patterns and charming mosaics, which normally we can only see from afar or behind a protective glass case.

But as we wander through each room, the artifacts themselves—ranging from incredibly detailed Greek pottery to colorful tomb paintings like nothing we have ever seen—manage to capture our attention even more than the floors. The *Magna Graecia* exhibit centers around the Greek colonization of Southern Italy, which occurred from the end of the eighth century BC until the Romans conquered the area in the third century BC, as well as the interaction of the Greek immigrants with the native Italic populations. It is a fitting herald of our upcoming flight to Athens in two days.

The rest of the museum is as wonderful as we remember, and we spend a few more hours admiring the extensive collections of painted frescoes, mosaics, pottery, and sculpture. We can hardly believe that, with the amount of artifacts housed in the museum, there can be anything left in Pompeii.

Because, of course, Pompeii is our final destination in Naples, and of the Italian leg of our journey as a whole. The following morning, we set out early from our hotel in Naples to board the train to Pompeii, thinking that perhaps if we arrive at the time the archaeological park opens we will miss the crowds. We are wrong. The train lines to Pompeii are packed, and we are dreading the crowds that we will have to push through down the ankle-breaking ancient Roman streets.

But when we make it inside the park, the crowds break off into clumps of tour groups, and we are nearly the only visitors to enter the famed House of the Faun before any of the tours begin. Shockingly, the streets of Pompeii feel empty. We see the *Cave Canem* mosaic without any trouble, visit the Villa of the Mysteries without a long line, and by the time we circle around to the main parts of town, it seems clear to us that the tour groups keep to a strict circuit and move on quickly. It's either that, or all of the tourists we saw at the Colosseum made the rational choice and booked it to the Amalfi Coast without bothering to visit any more 2000-year-old ruins.

8.4 The forum of Pompeii

Although we actually visited Pompeii twice during our time at the Centro (and indeed, to see the entire park thoroughly, one would and could spend several days there), we are surprised to find a house that was only very recently opened to the public. This is the House of the Vettii, and it is one of the most luxurious and well-preserved houses we have ever seen. Owned by two wealthy Roman freedmen, Aulus Vettius Conviva and Aulus Vettius Restitutus, the house is famed for its frescoes, many of which still survive from floor to ceiling.

The lower parts of the walls are painted to appear as if covered in marble, and the buildings depicted in the upper parts create the illusion that the walls have disappeared and the room stretches out into open space. In the middle of several of the walls, there are square panels portraying scenes from mythological stories, like Theseus abandoning the Cretan princess Ariadne and the eternal punishment of Ixion in the Underworld. The fresco that charms us the most is a frieze of little Cupids who are carrying out various tasks, like making flower garlands, pounding metal, and selling perfume to a female customer.

In one of the wings of the house, tucked in a back corner, is a small room. Each wall has painted in a small rectangle an erotic scene between a man and woman. It is difficult for us to imagine why the owner would choose such explicit scenes to adorn a room in his house. We think back to the exhibit on lamps in Pompeii, which we saw at the Capitoline Museum only a few days ago. As we imagine the room lit by a lamp, its light casting a seductive glow, only half-illuminating the teasing, twisting figures, we think we might understand the appeal if this was indeed a bedroom. After all, even today there is not much else that sets the scene like lighting a candle. And as for the erotic paintings, well, you get the point...

As we make our way through the houses we want to revisit (and this turns out to go rather quickly, given that many of them are unfortunately closed for restoration), we could not help but compare Pompeii to Ostia Antica, which we visited earlier in the week. In size, Pompeii is estimated at about 66 hectares with only two-thirds (approximately 44 hectares) excavated; the city of Ostia Antica now displays a similar 32 hectares of excavated ruins out of the 50 hectares that it encompasses in total. Interestingly, despite Ostia Antica's slightly smaller size, we feel as though there was much more to see in every nook and alley, whereas Pompeii's advantage lies partly in its signage and tourism organization.

We wonder why Pompeii, of course a very fascinating site in its own right, would garner more attention and tour groups than the equally expansive and fascinating Ostia Antica. We have come to two conclusions. The first: houses. While Ostia Antica has as much to offer as Pompeii, the latter boasts of large, luxury houses containing wall paintings, extremely well-preserved thanks to the volcanic eruption, that cover some houses from floor to ceiling. On the other hand, Ostia Antica was mainly a commercial and port city and preserved more fascinating public buildings and apartment complexes. Similar to our fascination with shows on HGTV and Sunday open-houses, stepping into the decorated mansions of Pompeii with beautiful gardens feels somewhat like touring a house and trying to imagine where to put the furniture. Even we cannot help but point out where a slim Roman bed would fit perfectly in a bedroom or how the light shines down beautifully on the garden in the center of a courtyard.

The Romans who occupied these homes were the elite of their society, fully staffed and owning slaves, and their lifestyles do not reflect how the majority of people lived at the time, such as those who would have rented rooms in the several stories of less-luxurious apartments stacked above these elegant houses. But nonetheless, we still enjoy wandering through their homes, admiring the wall paintings (essentially our modern wall-paper)

8.5 Inner courtyard of the House of the Vettii in Pompeii

and mosaics and marble-tiled floors (equivalent to hardwood floors and tiled bathrooms), as if, in the mere act of being in the space, we might imagine for a moment what it would feel like to live in that kind of luxury.

While there is certainly a level of fascination with cultural differences, such as their narrow beds, mythological painted scenes, and the small sizes of their rooms, the awe we feel, it seems, is mainly at the wealth and power that is signaled through the detailed paintings and precisely-cut mosaic tiles. As much as the bright blues and reds and the gold and bronze are artistically and aesthetically impressive, they also point to the wealth necessary to acquire those materials from the far reaches of the empire and the countless craftsmen hired to fashion them. This is as true today as it was then.

The second reason why Pompeii is more popular than Ostia Antica, and perhaps the reason nearer the point, is the manner of preservation. As we have experienced in Rome and other former Roman provinces, the story told about a place is essential in shaping how we see it. While Ostia Antica slowly fell to ruins, abandoned over the centuries, Pompeii was preserved in a tragic disaster: the eruption of Mount Vesuvius. Nearly everyone knows this story well, and as we walk the streets of Pompeii, we notice that the tour guides spend less time explaining archeological facts and more time repeating the story, mentioning the single, pivotal day after several centuries of history when everything fell dramatically to ruin. Tour groups even pause at body casts (the physical bodies long ago decayed, leaving imprints in the ash), discussing the positions of the victims at the time of the eruption.

One such body cast has a woman lying face-down, her dress pushed up to her waist from the explosion, preserving the exact moment of her death. It seems too personal, too tragic—one could argue even too immoral—to be so displayed. But at the end of the day, what draws many people to Pompeii is not the frescoes and mosaics alone but the tragedy that surrounds the city and our fascination with such an environmental disaster. While one may also see very beautiful artwork and architecture at Ostia Antica, the city does not have a story, at least not one that is shaped by such dramatic tragedy. This reason may also be the same one lurking behind our fascination with the underwater ruins of Baiae. It is not so much the actual mosaics and statues that we saw at those sites which drew us to them, but their state of preservation under the water and the eerie way in which the water encapsulates a time and place, like an ever-blooming rose trapped in a glass jar; not quite dead, but not alive either.

The environmental disaster, the tragedy of it all, feels like a metaphor for our own lives and times, and the role of Mother Earth in the granting of life—and the taking it away—that so troubles us. And while the sea may swallow the edges of a town, and a volcano may engulf an entire city, in the death of these places there is also permanence. Just like the Colosseum of Rome, or Ostia Antica covered in wild, overgrown grasses, or even the Neolithic stones in Évora, these ruins find meaning and life even after they have long been buried and abandoned, whether as testaments to a grand civilization, a new home for fish and barnacles, or simply a reflection of our own humanity. They remind us that all of our history, all of our cultures and cities, all of our monuments and art, belong ultimately to nature, as do we.

ATHENS & AEGINA

A WINE-DARK PAST

Let there be light! Said Liberty, And like sunrise from the sea, Athens arose!
—Percy Bysshe Shelley

Ancient of days! august Athena! where,
Where are thy men of might? thy grand in soul?
Gone—glimmering through the dream of things that were;
First in the race that led to glory's goal,
They won, and pass'd away—Is this the whole?
—Lord Byron

νῦν δ' ὧδε ξὺν νηὶ κατήλυθον ἠδ' ἑτάροισιν
πλέων ἐπὶ οἴνοπα πόντον ἐπ' ἀλλοθρόους ἀνθρώπους.

And now I have arrived with my ship and companions,
sailing upon the wine-dark sea to men who speak a foreign tongue.
–Homer, *Odyssey* 1.182–83

OUR FIRST DAY IN Greece is the hottest day of the year, nearly reaching 110°F. We already planned to go to the Acropolis, but we figure if we get there before it opens we will be in and out before the heat cranks up. As usual, everyone else had the same idea. The bus drops us off near the entrance, and even a few blocks away we can see the massive line forming. That isn't even the line to *buy* tickets. We ask a tour guide in line to double check, and sure enough, we have to wait in a separate line to buy them before rejoining the entrance line which has by now reached a major intersection down the block.

By chance, an older couple—Don and Jean, we find out later—overhear the tour guide pointing us to the correct line. It turns out they hadn't bought their tickets either, and they were in the wrong line. As we wait for the infinitely slow line to inch forward, Don and Jean, who are also American, strike up a conversation with us. They are in Greece for their 56th anniversary, they tell us, and have just come from Istanbul. We tell them about our trip and the blog, and they are delighted with our itinerary.

After we get our tickets, we feel sad to leave the lovely couple behind, joking that it felt like having another set of grandparents, and how we wanted them to adopt us. It is exhausting to look after yourself in a foreign country, and talking with them reminded us that we were still very young to pretend to be independent travelers. As if they heard us, Don and Jean find us in line and ask if they can join our party and joke about adopting us. We pass the time quickly in conversation, and soon enough, we are walking past the entrance gate.

But once we get inside and take the road up to the Acropolis, Don and Jean walk on up ahead—"I only want to get in, take a photo, then leave," says Jean, as this is their last day in Greece—while we linger at the ruins along the road and take photos of the Theater of Dionysus. Everything, however, changes drastically as we pass the Odeon and approach the Acropolis. The crowds of people in line to enter have come to a stop as the way up bottlenecks into a thin walkway and a two-by-two path through the ancient entryway.

We cannot see Don and Jean anywhere, and we hope they made it into the Acropolis, since the crowds of people stand close together, intensifying the heat. People desperately wave fans and shake out their clothes as the crowd inches forward at a painfully slow pace. We even see one young woman sitting on the side of the path, eyes half closing, suffering what we think is a heat stroke. Suddenly she collapses from her perch against the wall and people nearby shout for medical help. One woman even gives up her expensive-looking electric fan to aid the woman. It is a reminder that the heat can be one of the most dangerous elements, and should not be underestimated.

We are grateful to finally enter through the Propylaea, the monumental gates to the Acropolis, and spread out. The sun shines hot on the sand-and-stone peak, reflecting off all the white marble around us, but even this environment is better than being stuck in a crowd. Our route takes us to the Temple of Athena Nike first, dedicated to the goddess specifically in her role as a victor in war.

We then wander through the remains of the Sanctuary of Artemis Brauronia and, moving north across the Acropolis, marvel at the spot where the colossal bronze statue of Athena Promachos (*Promachos* is the ancient Greek word for "at the front lines of battle") once stood. It would be nice to be able to go back in time and see the statue in this spot, we think, but not on a day like today, when the sun is beating down so hard that the reflection of its light off of anything bronze would be nearly blinding.

We next make our way to the Old Temple of Athena (i.e., built before the Parthenon) and Erechtheion, pausing to see the Caryatids and the olive tree believed to have been gifted to the Athenians by Athena herself—never, of course, replanted in the thousands of years since that event. And after passing by the remains of a few more small sanctuaries, we come at last to the front of the Parthenon. While Zoë has visited the Acropolis before, this is Grace's first time in Athens, and the imposing size of the temple nearly takes her breath away. It is impossible not to feel the sanctity inherent in the site, not to stand in awe of its majesty.

But because of the heat, we have to tear ourselves away. After climbing down from the Acropolis, we buy two cups of frozen strawberry lemonade to sustain ourselves for the walk to the Acropolis Museum, which, with the temperature ever increasing, feels much longer than the 10 minutes that Google Maps promises us it will take. Once inside the modern, air-conditioned museum, we take a moment to cool down before exploring all it has to offer. The museum, which opened relatively recently in 2009, contains what feels like hundreds of artifacts found on the Acropolis; never before have we seen so many statues of Athena in one building.

Our favorite part of the museum is a section where ancient statues are presented alongside replicas that have been painted to show what the original looked like, before time and the elements weathered away the decorations. There is one statue of a *korē*, the ancient Greek term for a young girl, whose painted peplos we like so much that, after our visit, we buy paper fans from the museum gift shop with the same pattern on it. Another statue, called the Persian Rider, depicts a man on horseback. Only the legs of the man survive, but on his trousers are traces of paint that show a pattern of blue, red, and yellow diamonds, a depiction of fabric.

9.1 Loom with weights

It is not, however, simply the pretty hues and designs that make the exhibit so striking to us. It serves as a reminder that ancient Athens was visually vibrant, the artwork throughout the city full of color and details. What remains of the past in Athens today are the monumental buildings and statues of white marble. But the fabric painted on the statues, now so often invisible, recalls the work of women in ancient Greece, whose task it was to weave for the family. Indeed, one of the first things we saw upon entering the Acropolis Museum was a display case with a massive pile of spindles, as well as several loom weights, testifying to the widespread and essential role of weaving in the ancient world. While it may have been men who created the monuments and the history that define the modern-day memory of ancient Athens, it was the women who were responsible for creating the beauty, the fabric, of ancient Greek society, both literally and figuratively.

The following day of our trip brings the next museum on our list: the National Archaeological Museum of Athens, which is notably less crowded than the Acropolis Museum had been. The museum is laid out in chronological order, beginning with artifacts from various Neolithic settlements in Greece. Then we move to the Cycladic section. The culture of the Cycladic islands in the Aegean Sea became unified during the early Bronze Age (ca. 3200–2000 BC) and spread throughout many areas of Greece—the mainland, the eastern Aegean, and Crete—as the Cycladic civilizations were skilled sailors and traders. The Neolithic gold ornaments and finely-decorated Cycladic pottery lend nuance to our understanding of Greece's past: even in prehistoric times, this has been a place where wealth concentrated, different cultures mixed and spread, and art flourished.

Exiting the Cycladic exhibit, we are immediately confronted with hoards of Mycenaean gold, first of all the famous 'Mask of Agamemnon.' We can do nothing but marvel as we walk through the rooms and pass by cases of jewelry, armor, and other objects made, more than two millennia ago, of gleaming gold. The pure wealth radiating from each glass exhibit is more than surreal; it is so striking it feels unsettling, as hoards of gold come with death and burial, and we cannot help but wonder about these elite Mycenaeans, their treasure hoards meant never to see the light again, and how much wealth a single family must have had to bury so much of it away.

In addition to the masterpieces of Greek statuary, on the second floor of the museum there is a small exhibit with artifacts from Akrotiri, a small settlement on the island of Thera (modern-day Santorini) that was buried under ash during a volcanic eruption in 1600 BC—like Pompeii was, but about seventeen centuries earlier. As a result, there are preserved pieces of pottery, traces of furniture, and artwork. Our favorites are the frescoes, showing scenes with nature and people: a glimpse of real life 3500 years ago. After walking around the town of Pompeii in all its preserved glory and finding it so captivating, we can hardly wrap our minds around a similar town still decorated with such beautiful frescoes that lived its height nearly 2000 years earlier than our Pompeii. Coming to Greece feels like stepping off the coast of Italy and plunging into the depths of time, where 2000 years can be shrugged off without a thought. Italy suddenly seems young in comparison, and Greece much, much farther away. The thought tires us, and to lighten the burden of several millennia of history we grab lunch and a coffee at the cafe before leaving.

Once we exit the museum, we decide to look into a few bookstores that Google Maps tells us are nearby. But as we walk around, we quickly realize that not only does every block have a bookstore or two, but it seems every street has several, sometimes right next to each other, and we are completely overwhelmed. One would be entirely devoted to Greek, one to English, one even to French, while others seem to be more academic, others more like your traditional bookstore, still yet others devoted to used books. We have a hard time understanding how all of these bookstores are staying in business, especially with the intense competition all around, since Barnes & Nobles and other bookstores are notoriously running out of business in the United States.

We are reminded that at some point in time, the fact that Athens is so concerned with literature and education would not be so surprising. In the time of Plato and Aristotle, philosophy and tragedy were important facets of society and learning how to be a good citizen. But now, it is slightly surprising that Athens provides for so many small, independent bookstores. Are we surprised because of Greece's more recent history? One of the first things you learn about the Acropolis, after all, is that it was bombed in war and almost completely destroyed—as well as converted into a mosque and a church at different times, destroying more than preserving its ancient past. The city of Athens, after all, did not wander uneventfully from Classical Greek philosophers like Plato and Aristotle to the present day. Much happened in between then and now, which has greatly shaped their culture, language, and identity. Yet the abundance of bookstores suggests a continued preoccupation with learning and the spread of knowledge, which defies the belief that the younger generations today—perhaps thanks to the advent of social media—no longer care to read anymore.

Later that day, we get dinner with two of Zoë's classmates from college. It is their last night in Athens before flying back to the US. One of them is in fact a fellow Classics major, and he asks about some of the sites we have seen (they had just a week earlier boldly climbed Mount Olympus, though apparently caught no sight of Zeus' lofty halls). This is the first dinner we are having with other people and it is a delightful change in pace to feel social and break up the string of archeological sites and museums. But we can't be away from the ancient world for too long, so after dinner we head up to a rooftop bar with a view of the Acropolis, the Parthenon lit up against the black night sky. It feels like gazing up at Mount Olympus, where heroes and gods mingle, despite the fact that the ancients would never have seen the temples lit up by fluorescent lights. From the rooftop bar, decked out with flowers and blasting house music, and surrounded by youthful, dolled up faces, the Acropolis and its nearly 5000 years of history feels far away, almost untouchable. We get the sense that perhaps it is meant to feel like that, both then and now.

In antiquity, the Acropolis was where Athens conducted its religious worship and stored its wealth. Now, it is a tourist site, symbolically linking the present Greek society to its ancient past, ignoring centuries of history, especially the occupation by the Ottoman Empire. It is so very different to Rome and its Colosseum, which stands firmly on the ground, close enough to touch, nearly grazed by the countless passing buses each day. They call Rome a lasagna for a reason, its many layers visible at all times from antiquity to the Middle Ages to the years of fascism under Mussolini, if one only looks down the street. Rome's ancient history is brought closer to you, enlarged and glorified but still very human, and even its emperors, though deified, are portrayed more like royalty than anything else. Yet in Athens, this is not so. The ancient past is raised up, overlooking the city in all its pride. Below it, the sea of white apartments and buildings built quickly and cheaply in the 1950s,

9.2 The Erechtheion on the Acropolis

bustling with traffic and commuters and tourists, is set firmly in the present, mere mortals in comparison to the larger-than-life figures who once walked this earth, who now only live in a legendary past.

The next morning, we visit the ancient Athenian Agora, as well as the Roman Agora and Hadrian's Library, hoping to feel as though we could imagine life in Ancient Greece more clearly. This is not exactly the case, however, and we find ourselves feeling the same as we did on the Acropolis. This lack of concrete understanding only further intensifies as we come upon the statue of Socrates standing beside a statue of Confucius, who were two great thinkers living around the same time in history, though their lifetimes did not overlap. The statues were made by Wu Weishan and dedicated in Greece in 2021 in celebration of the Greece-China Year of Culture and Tourism. The two figures seem to be mid-conversation in an impossible dialogue, and it throws into sharp relief how much globalization has changed the world today. While the ancient world was certainly more connected and well-traveled than we often realize, we now recognize our shared humanity more readily, and we can look at both Socrates and Confucius, two of the greatest philosophers to ever live, and claim them as our world's heritage.

The next day is our last day in Athens, but we are actually visiting the island of Aegina. It takes a metro and a ferry to reach the island, but we are surprised by how accessible it is to get there. The ferry ride is beautiful, and the waters of the Saronic gulf spread around us in a calm teal blue. This immediately strikes us as very funny.

"Why did Homer ever describe the water as *wine-dark?*" we ask ourselves.

"It's as bright blue as a Gatorade," Grace jokes. "Or a heavily chlorinated pool."

It is probable that the word οἶνοψ, which we often translate as 'wine-dark,' merely meant 'blue' to the ancient Greeks. Or it simply referred to their version of wine, which was always watered down. Either way, it is funny that the English translation (ironically a very Germanic-sounding compound word) would come to represent the ancient Greek world in our imaginations, yet appear at utter odds with the nearly turquoise waters we see today. It makes us laugh to think of Odysseus lost at sea—not a terrifying, wine-dark sea hiding monstrous creatures—but a warm, clear, light-blue sea, inviting in its calm waves and glittering sand below. Clearly, we think, we know nothing of the past and the ancient Greeks if *this* is the ocean they sailed upon.

All too soon we arrive on the island of Aegina, which is even more beautiful than the waters that surround it. Our first stop is the archaeological site of Kolona, where the ancient acropolis of the city once held a temple to Apollo, of which only one column still stands today—hence the name 'Kolona,' the Greek word for 'column.' It is a small site with an even smaller museum, and afterwards we head to the car rental office, where we will pick up the car we have reserved and drive across the island to our next stop. The owner of the rental cars, however, tells us that there are no automatic cars available—the only two automatic cars were taken by a large British family and he has no idea when they would return today. But our ferry is in three hours and we have much to see.

"Can you drive stick?" he asks.

"No," we both answer hurriedly.

"Americans," he mutters in disappointment. "You are all the same."

At this, Zoë glances at the ATVs lined up by the wall. She had spent many summers and Christmases in Northern California driving quads on the dirt paths of Paso Robles. "How about one of those?"

9.3 Coastline of the island of Aegina with the archeological site of Kolona in the distance

It turns out that driving an ATV on the empty roads of Paso would not hold a candle to driving on Greek island roads. While we had been warned of the recklessness of Greek drivers, what we were not told was that there are actually a few strict rules that *must* be followed. Essentially, if you are going slower than the car behind you, it is not only a courtesy but *expected* that you lean closer to the right and give them room to pass quickly and safely before oncoming traffic approaches. Not only that, but you must also drive slower in order to give them time to pass you. While we thought this might only apply to us driving slow and careful in an ATV, we quickly learned that all drivers know this, and even other fast Greek cars would submissively inch to the right to allow a much faster car to pass them.

Other than that, the drive up to our next stop is more or less smooth, and besides our occasional pauses to catch our breath and recheck our place on the map ("No navigation tools on an ATV," we mutter, thinking wistfully about that air-conditioned automatic car), we arrive at the temple of Aphaia without incident. This temple is an interesting site, since this is the only known place in the ancient world where the goddess Aphaia—a fertility goddess of Cretan origin—was worshiped. The view is worth the trek up to the top of the mountain, and we stare at the sea on both sides. By the time we return the ATV to the shop, we are exhausted and mildly sunburnt. It is time to have a taste of that wine-dark sea for ourselves. The beach near the marina is beautiful and just slightly crowded. We swim out in the water, and sure enough, it is warm and clear to the bottom, free of sirens and sea monsters. Unfortunately, our high-speed ferry leaves in thirty minutes, and we have to say goodbye to Aegina and her warm waters. Our last event in Athens is soon approaching, and it is not something we want to miss.

We return to Athens, and after a quick pit stop at the Benaki Museum, we get ready for a night at the opera, which will be performed in the Odeon—a type of small theater where music and poetry was performed—carved into the slope of the Acropolis. We are seeing the opera *Nabucco*, which was composed in 1841 by Giuseppe Verdi to an Italian libretto that had been written by Temistocle Solera. The plot, based on a narrative from the Old Testament, sets a story of love and jealousy against religious conflict between the Israelites and Babylonians in the 6th century BC. While the marble seats, which contain only thin cushions, are uncomfortable to sit on for the nearly three-hour duration of the opera, it is nonetheless magical to watch a performance in such an ancient space as the crescent moon shines above the stage.

It is a lovely end to our time in Athens, and although the ancient world and its pale gleaming ruins feel even farther away in Greece, we find that the beautiful voices of the opera and their tragic, nearly comic deaths on such an old stage ultimately link us to all those who came before, even if we cannot quite imagine the lives they once led.

9.4 Nabucco performed in the Odeon at night

THE GREEK MAINLAND

Prophetic Journies

And thence from Athens turn away our eyes, To seek new friends and stranger companies.
—Shakespeare, *A Midsummer Night's Dream*

Among all peoples, the Greeks have dreamt life's dream most beautifully.
–Goethe

The Greeks had a sense of the magic truth of things. Thank goodness one still knows enough about them to find one's kinship at last.
—D.H. Lawrence, *Sea and Sardinia*

AFTER FOUR DAYS IN Athens, we are ready to leave. Despite the grandeur of the Acropolis and her temples and the bustling, lively city life, thanks to the lingering heatwave, crowds, and stuffy public transit, we have something to look forward to on our way out. Because our journey is not over: we have one last road trip before heading home.

We pick up our rental car at the Athens Airport. Although we have been warned about Greek drivers by well-meaning family and friends, Zoë finds that navigating city traffic as we pass Athens is not unlike her high school commute on the 405 freeway in Los Angeles. By the time we turn onto the highway on our way to Thebes, the cars are fewer, and with the music turned up, it starts to feel like a real roadtrip. While we make a brief stop in Thebes to see the recently constructed archeological museum there (which is worth a visit for anyone interested in Classics), the day's destination is Delphi, the site of the ancient oracle.

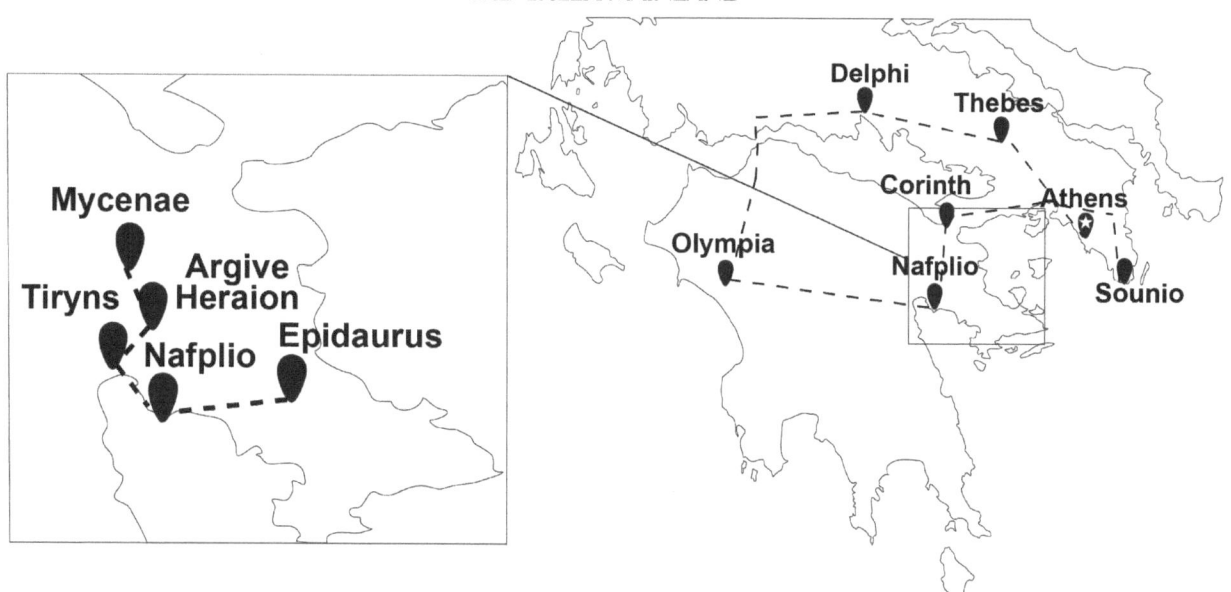

10.1 Map of Greece and our planned road trip route

The drive up to Delphi into the mountains is magical, and as the vineyards and farmlands fade to rocky out-croppings and treacherous ravines, we turn quiet and pensive. Many people in the ancient world would have trekked up this road to the lofty peaks where Delphi rests, hoping for an answer to their questions, and as the valley falls below us and we catch far-off glimpses of the blue ocean, it is not surprising why they considered the site prophetic.

"If you could ask the oracle one question, what would it be?" Grace asks.

"Hmm...how about...who am I going to marry?" Zoë jokes.

While this may sound trite, you might (or might not) be surprised by how many ancient Greeks asked the oracle about happiness with their future spouses...

However, we do not visit the site today. Instead, with the new freedom our car has granted us, we joyfully drive the twenty minutes to the nearest beach in Itea after checking into our hotel. The beach chairs and umbrellas are surprisingly packed with young people and families vacationing, and the café bar nearby blasts pop music. We sip our Freddo Cappuccinos and take a dip in the warm waters. At long last, this trip is starting to feel like a vacation.

That night we have dinner at a restaurant in Delphi (which, incidentally, is named *In Delphi*), at the corner of the two one-way streets which are the only ways in and out of the town from the east entrance. Outside in the middle of the road are three enormous stray dogs who look more like wolves. They are not afraid of the cars passing inches from them, and they even bark at a few that drive by, as if to show that they own the place. It certainly looks like they do. Zoë, in fact, had previously met one of these dogs on her first visit to Delphi last January, and her classmates had joked that he was Apollo in dog-form—only to find out that he had indeed been given the name Apollo by some of the townspeople. But when Zoë asks the waiter for their names, he shakes his head. It turns out they are given many names, because they are stray dogs without a home.

"It is very sad," our Greek waiter says, looking at the dogs. He started working at Delphi only a weekend prior, and before that he had been living in London for a time. "You don't see that in other places. Dogs left on the street like that. It is not civilized."

We look at the dogs, who lounge in the shade of the trees near the restaurant tables where, we suppose, they are more likely to find a scrap of food. Although it is always sad to see dogs without homes, it seems to us that these dogs have known a special freedom and community roaming the small town of Delphi, finding cool places to lie down and grassy areas to explore, even visiting the archeological site. Tourists love the dogs, giving them water and food and petting them. There are countless cats, too, who prowl up and down the tall terraces, often keeping the dogs company. It is hard to imagine these animals locked up in a house, even if that would offer them constant care and attention, as if they are now one with the landscape, one with the small streets and ancient stones.

Early the next morning, we set out from our hotel and prepare to visit the oracle. Before climbing the slope up to the sanctuary, we first stop at the site of the Castalian Spring, where pilgrims in antiquity would cleanse themselves before ascending. Though all that remains of the spring now is foundations, there is a water fountain just a few meters away, and we fill up our water bottles before we make the climb. The water definitely tastes like it came out of a mountain, and we feel that we have done our due diligence to the ancient rites.

For the Greeks and Romans, the Sanctuary of Apollo at Delphi was the site of the most important oracle in the world: the Pythia. The Pythia was a priestess of Apollo who supposedly communicated with the god and could reveal his will—but she only took consultations for a few days per year, so it was imperative to plan well in advance if you wanted to ask her something. The Pythia's oracles were famously ambiguous, given not as simple words but in hexameter verse, and could mislead one to the wrong actions unless they analyzed them thoroughly.

Because the site was so well frequented by people from all over the known world, many Greek city-states competed to show off their wealth by building monuments and treasuries along the Sacred Way, the path leading to the temple of Apollo that anyone who wanted to consult the Pythia or go to the sanctuary's theater or stadium had to take. The Sacred Way, now more of a dirt path than a road, offers us gorgeous vistas over the mountains and valley, but in antiquity our view would instead have been of bronze and marble statuary and treasuries filled with gold objects.

10.2 The archeological site at Delphi above the remains of the Temple of Apollo

Although the view takes our breath away, the most prominent feature of our hike up to the stadium at the very top of the site are the bees. They range in different sizes and colors, species and sounds, honey bees and wasps and everything in between. Not only are they very active, flying from tree to tree and exploring the vast grounds of the site, but they are also curious, especially about the tourists, and more than once Zoë (who is irrationally terrified of bees) is scared half to death as yet another bee buzzes up beside her dress, which was unfortunately printed with bright, inviting yellow flowers.

The phenomenon of bees at Delphi makes it easy for us to understand why the ancient Greeks associated prophecy with bees. The ancient Homeric Hymn to Hermes tells of three bee-women who live under a ridge of Mt. Parnassus and taught Apollo the gift of prophecy. In fact, the second version of the temple at Delphi (after the first one was destroyed) was said to have been built by bees, who used feathers and beeswax for construction material. Pindar, a lyric poet of the 5th century BC from Thebes, even wrote an ode in which he calls the Pythia the 'Delphic Bee.' It surely is no surprise, and as we make the connection with the Greek obsession with honey, we realize that honey, after all, might not have been so different from the gods' beloved ambrosia.

In the afternoon, after another Freddo Cappuccino and peach iced tea (attracting more wasps, one of which boldly entered the glass and nearly drowned in the sweet drink), we begin the long three-hour drive to Olympia. The route swings us by the coast, and we are in awe of the turquoise water hugging the rugged cliffside. Zoë remarks that the groves of gnarled trees and vineyards backdropped by mountains and coastal views would not look so out of place in California. But once we roll into Olympia, the signs direct us to the town near the ancient site, and we are pulled back into the depths of Greek history.

We are not sure what to expect from the modern town of Archaia Olympia, where we are staying just a few minutes' walk from the archaeological site, but its size (or, rather, its lack thereof) still manages to surprise us when we arrive. The downtown area is no more than four or five blocks, and it seems that at least two-thirds of the stores lining every street are tourist shops, selling replicas of Greek vases or t-shirts branded with temples. Archaia Olympia appears to be a town that exists primarily to serve visitors of the archaeological site, which perhaps should not surprise us at all: the ancient Olympic Games were held every four years, just as the modern Olympics are, but unlike the games we know today, the ancient Greek Olympics were held not in various major cities but always at the sanctuary of Zeus in Olympia. The ancient town of Olympia, thus, would only serve the athletes and spectators of the games, not dissimilar to the modern town that seems to exist merely for us tourists.

In order to take advantage of the cooling temperatures of the late evening, we decide to visit the archaeological site of Olympia soon after we arrive, wandering around the palaestra where πάλη, Doric πάλα, "wrestling," was taught and also performed. In the shaded courtyard, lined by columns, we can just envision the naked torsos gleaming with sweat as they wrestle across the grassy lawn, spectators cheering them on. Passing by the statue bases of the *Zanes*—bronze statues of Zeus that athletes caught cheating had to pay for and put their names on (cheating in athletics, it seems, is not a modern phenomenon)—we also visit the track where runners would race and crowds of entirely naked and mostly drunk men would shout and bet on who would win. Now all that remains is a stretch of dust and dirt surrounded by green slopes, the smells and noise of the games a distant reality, for which we were grateful in this case. But as we watch other tourists attempt to run the track all the way to the finish line, for a brief second the triumph and glory of winning such a race flashes before our eyes, still commemorated in the modern-day Olympics but never reaching the same heights of divine glory.

Ultimately, we can catch only glimpses of the site's former grandeur. At the Temple of Zeus, all that remains are crumbling stone columns, though massive in diameter, to testify to the fact that this building was once worthy of housing one of the Seven Wonders of the Ancient World: the statue of Olympian Zeus. Our guidebook informs us that the statue, over 40 feet tall and constructed of ivory and gold, was made in the fifth century by Phidias, a famed scultpor who drew artistic inspiration for the project from Homer's descriptions of Zeus, the regal but terrifying father and king of the gods, in the *Iliad*. But sometime after the fourth century AD, the statue was stolen and destroyed, and now we can only use our imaginations to reconstruct the statue of the fearsome god as we gaze upon the ruins of his temple, a light blue evening sky behind it.

The ancient Olympics undoubtedly celebrated masculine athelticism, but when we wander from the archaeological site to the nearby antiquarium we realize that we might be able to see ourselves, too, in the history of the competition. In one of the antiquarium's glass display cases is an unassuming stone that once served as a statue base, inscribed with the following lines:

> *Kings of Sparta are my father and brothers*
> *I, Cynisca, victorious with a chariot of swift-footed horses,*
> *have erected this statue. I declare myself the only woman*
> *in all Hellas to have won this crown.*
> *Apelleas son of Kallikles made it.*

In 396 BC, the Spartan princess Cynisca became the first woman ever to receive the title of 'Olympic victor'. Though as a woman, she was barred from physically competing in any athletic competitions, she used her wealth to commission a team of horses and charioteer to compete on her behalf. As we reach the end of the site, hot and exhausted from being on foot for several hours under a Greek summer sun, we imagine the Spartan princess sitting on the shaded sidelines yet still winning a crown. Cynisca was a smart woman, we think.

By the next morning, we realize there is not much else to do in the town. So we drive to our next destination: the popular vacation port city of Nafplio. After a picturesque dinner on the waterfront at Nafplio, we drive the half hour to the Sanctuary of Asclepius at Epidaurus. The drive is breathtaking as we cross the Argolid, mountains and valleys sweeping across the land, broken up by tall, looming outcrops of sheer gray, which have lit up in a hot red glow from the sunset. We have tickets for an event that we've been looking forward to for months. We are seeing a performance of Aristophanes' *Frogs*—an ancient Greek comedy first performed in 405 BC—in the theater of Epidaurus, one of the most famous and well-preserved theaters from antiquity, renowned for its acoustics. In its original state from the 4th century BC, the theater could house 14000 spectators, something hard for us to believe as we cram into the seating, hip-to-hip with a mere 9000 other attendees.

The performance is more or less faithful to the ancient version, at least from the parts of the dialogue that we can comprehend. The actors speak in modern Greek with English subtitles that, unfortunately, appear only sporadically on the screens flanking the stage. But having read *Frogs* already, we can still follow along and understand what is going on: the god Dionysus descends to the Underworld intending to bring back the deceased Athenian playwright Euripides, but after a verbal competition between Aeschylus (another dead playwright) and Euripides, Dionysus decides that Aeschylus is more talented and brings him back up to earth. The name of the play, *Frogs*, comes from the chorus of the comedy, which is partly sung by frogs. Although these frogs are supposed to be a parody of a typical Greek chorus, as the crickets chirp away in the trees even louder than the music at times, we find that *Frogs* might not have been far from the truth.

During one of the scenes when the subtitles are thankfully working, we see Dionysus on stage giving a monologue about the importance of art for healing society. Indeed, the god Asclepius (whose sanctuary the theater stood next to) was the god of medicine and healing, and the ancient Greeks believed that people who visited the sanctuary to seek remedies for their afflictions could find at least some relief by attending performances at the theater. As we listen to the passionate verses of Dionysus, backlit by dark mountains and trees, the Big Dipper hanging in the sky above—a plane flies by, oblivious to the pivotal scene, oblivious to thousands of years of history—we think we might just understand what the god is saying.

The next morning, we make the same drive from our hotel in Nafplio back to Epidaurus to see the rest of the archaeological site. This time, we make only a quick pit-stop at the theater (we did spend a solid three hours sitting there last night, after all) before heading to the area of the sanctuary itself. The foundations of the massive temple to Asclepius remain, but what really interests us are the other types of buildings that we haven't seen at the other sanctuaries we've visited, such as Delphi and Olympia. The Greeks believed that, in order to be healed by Asclepius, one had to sleep in the *Enkoimeterion* (a porticoed space surrounding the temple) and would receive dreams from the god telling them how to resolve their illness. There are also the remains of several different hostels—some seeming nicer than others—where caretakers of the ill supplicants would presumably stay. While we are thankful for our modern-day doctors and hospitals, our dwindling supply of Advil and the cost of buying it in Greece makes us reconsider the benefits of a nap in a temple...

Our next site, Tiryns, takes us even further back in time. Tiryns is a fortress that was extremely powerful in the Mycenaean period. It was especially known for its walls—in the *Iliad*, Homer refers to it as 'well-walled Tiryns'—and this is still the main attraction today. The walls are called Cyclopean because, it is believed, they are so gigantic that they could only have been constructed by the mythical, incredibly strong Cyclopes. It is strange to stand atop the palace of a once-dominating city, which has now crumbled to its rocky foundations, hardly a hearth and columns visible in the throne room, and whose passing mention in Homer's epics leaves much to the imagination.

10.3 Theater of Epidaurus

By the end of our visit at Tiryns, the sun is beating down on us and it's time for lunch. We gratefully return to the cool waterfront restaurants of Nafplio before driving to a nearby beach cradled by the mountains on all sides. The water is warm but refreshing as we swim out into the shallows. Across the water more mountains loom in dark, misty shadows, and as the sun sets gently in the west, we realize our trip is truly coming to an end.

The following day is our second-to-last day, and we head early to the Argive Heraion, hoping to save more time later for a last beach day. Even though the morning is still young, the day is already hot, and we feel the rays of the sun on our faces as we climb up a steep dirt path to see the ruins of the temple and surrounding buildings. We feel lucky that we have a car to take us at least part of the way up the slope of the hill on which the Heraion stands, for the ancient Greeks would have walked as they conducted an annual procession of worshippers and sacrificial animals to the temple all the way from the town of Argos. As we gaze at the fertile valley below, reaching near to the blue bay, the land suddenly feels solemn and heavy, as if we may hear the procession coming up from Argos at any moment, livestock trudging in the dirt, bearing an ancient song like a whisper in the wind.

But we have saved the best for last: Mycenae. The drive deeper into the Argolid plain is winding and slow but stunning, and the climb up to the acropolis is tantalizing in its snatched views of wide open fields and slivers of blue waters. Soon the road inches up to the slopes where the palace of Mycenae is built on a high, rocky outcrop surrounded by dangerous, steep ravines. It is no wonder this site has been fortified for so long.

But before we go up to the palace, we stop by a large tomb, named the Treasury of Atreus but more popularly called the Tomb of Agamemnon. Perhaps the site where Agamemnon—king of Mycenae and one of the commanders of the Greeks in the Trojan War—was buried, this tomb contained hoards of gold treasure, which we have already seen in the National Archaeological Museum in Athens. The tomb itself has a large domed ceiling, and our footsteps echo against the bare blocks of stone like a heartbeat. It is eerie, and so we head up to the acropolis of Mycenae to see the famous Lion Gate and the palace.

Before we do, though, we stop by the two tombs located outside the acropolis, the so-called Tomb of Clytemnestra and the Tomb of Aegisthus, the former queen of Mycenae (and wife of Agamemnon) and her lover respectively. Inside the tomb of Clytemnestra, the world grows quiet and dark, and we wait, as if at any moment her ghost will appear in fury as it did to Orestes.

Grace gasps, pointing. Zoë turns, too scared to speak. But it is only a dog, pale blonde and curled up in the darkness, hardly distinguishable from the dusty dirt ground. The dog does not stir as we stare at it, not knowing what to say. It is hard to pinpoint exactly what about the scene makes us pause then shake our heads, except that animals at archaeological sites usually appear to be unaware of the history of the space, and yet this dog looks almost solemn, as if guarding the burial place of the queen. We quickly leave both the dog and Clytemnestra's tomb in peace to begin the march up to the acropolis.

10.4 The Lion's Gate of Mycenae

Mycenae was an incredibly important city in the ancient world, being a locus of trade and having a highly organized political system as well as enormous wealth. But even after its destruction in 1200 BC, its memory did not fade, since the Mycenean king Agamemnon is one of the main characters in Homer's *Iliad*. For the ancient Romans, in fact, Mycenae was a 'tourist site,' not unlike it is today. Perhaps the ancient Romans, like us, stopped and stared at the Lion's Gate, wondering if Agamemnon himself paused here on the way up to the palace after the Greek victory in the Trojan War, a beat of apprehension in his step, before walking to his death. And at the top of the palace, the world seemingly lying at its feet, would not have Clytemnestra, full of anger and pride, beckoned her husband there and ensnared him in her net? If that happened at all, it happened very long ago, and now all that remains are traces and legendary tales long turned to myth.

Once we have explored the site of Mycenae to our heart's content, we drive back to Nafplio, excited to revisit the same beach. It is harder, this time, to say goodbye, as this is our last night in Nafplio and our second-to-last night in Greece. We take a walk around the peninsula where a pathway is bordered by tall cliffs on one side and a sheer drop on the other, the waves of the Argolic gulf crashing against the rocks. The horizon is flanked by mountains cast in shadow by the setting sun, and it seems as we gaze upon it that the ocean does not continue but ends in a waterfall, falling off the edge of the earth. We wonder if this is what the ancient Greeks felt as they sailed from this port on their way to Troy, and this time it is not very hard to imagine Scylla in all her monstrous glory or the island of the Cyclopes just over the fog of the horizon.

Our last day comes quickly, as we wake up early to drive to our ultimate destination near the Athens airport, where we will spend our last night before our separate flights tomorrow. As we drive past endless fields and vineyards, with hardly the sight of a church nearby, suddenly there appears on the lofty heights of a grand outcropping a fortified wall, long since abandoned but still peering ominously on the valley below.

"Can you believe this place was important enough to need fortifications?" Zoë jokes, as they had been passing what felt like miles of farmland and scattered houses.

Grace looks at her map, then raises a brow. "Well, that's actually Corinth."

Specifically, it is the acropolis of Corinth, and we quickly find out that there is also an archeological site of the ancient town below. We cannot help ourselves, even though it was not in our plan, and before we know it we are pulling off the highway and driving up the precipitous, winding dirt road to the acropolis. What remains today of the fortress dates primarily to the reconstructions conducted by the Byzantines, Franks, and Venetians as each group took over the area in turn, but the high walls and imposing gates give us a sense of what it would have looked and felt like in antiquity. The acropolis commands views over the surrounding farmland and bays, and was in a strategic location where its occupants could control the Isthmus, the vital strip of land connecting the Peloponnese to the rest of the mainland.

Soon we tire of the steep, slippery stone roads of the acropolis (how anyone got all the way up there, much less *conquered* it, is a mystery) and head back down to the ancient site of Corinth, which, like Archaia Olympia, is surrounded by a few restaurants and tourist shops. But unlike Archaia Olympia, in the past Corinth was a flourishing, densely populated city. By the 8th century BC, it was already establishing colonies in such distant places as Syracuse, and during the Classical period it amassed huge amounts of wealth by controlling trade over the Isthmus as well as exporting black-figure pottery.

The Romans, however, brought that to an abrupt end. In 146 BC, the Roman army captured Corinth and destroyed the city, killing or enslaving its entire population. Not until 44 BC, when Julius Caesar re-founded it as a Roman colony, was there any sort of civilization in Corinth. But as a Roman town, it regained at least some of its former prestige, for it served as the administrative capital of the province of Achaea.

The main attraction of the site is the temple of Apollo, which was built in the 6th century and is actually one of the few archaic Greek temples that still stands today (most date to the Classical period or later). Other than this, the archaeological site is somewhat lacking in signage, and we have to make our best guesses as to what we are seeing as we walk around the site. By this point in our trip, though, we are well-versed in what the remains of a forum, a fountain, a temple, or a bath complex look like, and we leave the site with a sense of accomplishment that we have been able to identify parts of the site, if also with an incomplete image of ancient Corinth.

Once we begin driving to our hotel, it starts to settle in that we have only one more sight to see: the Temple of Poseidon at Sounion. After taking a much-needed rest, we drive down the coast to the temple. The view is, of course, breathtaking, endless sea upon endless sea, sharp, sloping mountains jutting out of the water, and the Temple of Poseidon standing as a pale lookout over the cliff's edge, a testament to the past as well as the future.

We watch the sun sink down below the mountains, hovering above their crests in a red-gold gleam, like the fading light of Helios' chariot, just before the full moon rises to bid us adieu. It is a good omen. Our journey ends here, but somehow, it doesn't feel like that. Just like the temple, we look forward to a rising sun.

10.5 Temple of Poseidon at Sounion

THE END OF AN ODYSSEY

Q&A

ἀλλ’ ἄγε μοι τόδε εἰπὲ καὶ ἀτρεκέως κατάλεξον,
ὅππῃ ἀπεπλάγχθης τε καὶ ἅς τινας ἵκεο χώρας
ἀνθρώπων, αὐτούς τε πόλιάς τ’ ἐὺ ναιετοώσας,
ἠμὲν ὅσοι χαλεποί τε καὶ ἄγριοι οὐδὲ δίκαιοι,
οἵ τε φιλόξεινοι, καί σφιν νόος ἐστὶ θεουδής.

And now, tell me and declare it truly.
Where have you been wandering, and to what countries
of men have you travelled? Tell us of the peoples themselves,
and of their cities—who were hostile, savage and unjust,
and who were hospitable and god-fearing.
—Homer, *Odyssey* 8.572–76

WE ARE PUBLISHING THIS volume two years after our trip, and since then much has happened—we both graduated college with degrees in Classics and began graduate programs focusing on the ancient world in different ways. When we both returned to our version of "home" before the next chapter of our lives, we took the time to reflect on our odyssey of a trip. As we hope this trip inspires others to embark on their own odysseys into the past, this chapter will individually answer some questions about the trip that may be helpful or illuminating for future time-travelers.

What was your favorite part of the trip?

Zoë: A tough question, but I have to say the road trip around Greece. Having a car gave us such freedom and comfort after taking so much public transit—in a heatwave no less. It might be cliché for a Californian and LA native to have enjoyed driving the most (as Grace so kindly pointed out) but having air conditioning, blasting our favorite music, and watching the drop-dead-gorgeous Greek countryside and coastal vistas unfold around us was unreal. Plus, besides access to far-off sites, it gave us a few much-needed beach days, which we couldn't have done without a car.

Grace: Does it make sense to say that my favorite part of the trip was the essence of the trip itself? While certain experiences definitely stand out as favorites, like scuba diving and the tour of Neolithic stones in Évora, ultimately I loved being able to just immerse myself in the physical environment of the ancient world for nearly five weeks straight.

What was the most disappointing part of the trip?

Zoe: I hate to say Italy, since it was the country I most looked forward to given it was where Grace and I met and went to the Centro together, which probably set my expectations too high. My fond memories of the Centro in the cooler fall season made this unbearably hot, crowded, and exhausting leg of the trip almost impossible. But it's still Italy, so the Cacio e Pepe, Hugo spritzes, and beautifully preserved Roman ruins certainly made up for the fact that we traveled to Italy during the worst month possible.

Grace: The most disappointing part was seeing that certain cities/sites, like Pompeii, the Athenian Acropolis, and Delphi, were very busy and well-frequented by tour groups, whereas others, like Ostia Antica, the Neolithic stones in Évora, and the Vatican's Etruscan Museum, had hardly any tourists. While I know that not everyone shares my and Zoë's passion for visiting museums and archaeological sites, it was a sad realization for me that sites which have so much fascinating information to offer, so many lessons to teach us, may never get the attention they deserve because people just don't know that they even exist.

If you could plan the trip over again, what would you change?

Zoë: More time in Italy. Even though it's hard to fix a heatwave or the outrageous crowds, more time to separate our numerous activities that we, in our mortal hubris, thought we could manage in a mere five days would have eased our time there. Alternatively, not visiting Ostia Antica and Palestrina could have helped, although those were some of our favorite sights so it would have been a painful decision nonetheless.

Grace: I would opt to rent a car for the majority of the trip, besides when we were in big cities like Rome and Athens that are more accessible by foot or public transportation. Having a car in Greece allowed us to visit so many out-of-the-way sites that are hard to access by public transit, and the ability to travel in an air-conditioned car and go places on our own schedule allowed us to relax a little bit. With a car in Portugal, Spain, and Italy, I think that we would have been able to fit more places into our itinerary and, at the same time, have a somewhat more relaxed experience.

What surprised you the most?

Zoë: Definitely Mérida, although nearly all of the sites on the Iberian Peninsula (special shout out to Conímbriga and Évora) were very surprising in what and how much is preserved. Italy and Greece tend to get more attention in Classical Studies, but Mérida has one of the best preserved theaters we have ever seen, a beautiful amphitheater, and some stunning mosaics, as attested in their awesome archeological museum.

Grace: I was (pleasantly) surprised by how enthralled I've become with Neolithic and Cycladic cultures. I'd not had much prolonged exposure to these time periods before our trip, and especially in Évora and Greece I was stunned to see just how many artifacts have survived and how much scholars know about those cultures. It was also eye-opening to realize how significant of an influence these prehistoric peoples had on Greco-Roman civilizations and cultures. This is a part of Classics that I'm excited to keep exploring, if only in an informal way. Plus, I have gained an intense, newfound love for Cycladic Greek art, which is a sentence that I never could have expected to write.

What was the hardest part of the trip?

Zoë: Honestly, besides some of the other things I've mentioned like heat, crowds, and walking nonstop for many, many miles, the hardest part ended up just being on the road for so long in a foreign country. While I love traveling and I have a special love for the countries we visited, I soon got tired of some culture shocks like poor restaurant service, limited medicinal options, and a lack of cold water. Also, not speaking some of the languages fluently and knowing very few people in most of the cities we visited created a more solitary experience, but at the same time it allowed us to follow our own schedule and visit the sites we wanted to.

Grace: For me, the hardest part was lacking time to really reflect on the sites as we visited them. Because we did a lot of things back-to-back, we often didn't have time to just sit and think deeply about what we were visiting until the end of the day. But that's why I'm glad we had our blog and these essays: not only did it give us the chance to reflect on our experiences, but it also preserves them as a record so that I can continue to think about them even as I'm physically and temporally removed from them.

What was the most beautiful place you visited?

Zoë: Can you really choose? I think Nafplio might take the prize for me on this trip. Even though Delphi's view is simply incredible and Portugal will always be the most beautiful country to me as a whole, I found my breath actually catching whenever we looked at the water surrounding Nafplio, and the beach we went to surrounded by mountains was particularly magical. However, Palestrina in Italy and Aegina in Greece are equally beautiful and will always hold a special place in my heart.

Grace: As Zoë said, Delphi's view is incredible, and in my opinion it was the most beautiful place we went to. The mountains were stunning, and I honestly lack the words to describe how much their appearance struck me. I also found the site itself particularly beautiful (yes, I genuinely find bare foundations of ancient buildings beautiful!). Its long history as a sacred place is very compelling to me and increased how much I loved the views. There was something special and deeply beautiful about being in a location where so many people have sought and received wisdom—and I think I found some answers of my own there.

What was your favorite archeological site? Museum?

Zoë: Again, hard to choose. While Greek sites often have the most breathtaking views, the Roman sites had the most beautifully preserved frescoes and mosaics. Not to mention the exciting new sites in Portugal and Spain, especially Conímbriga and Mérida. But for this trip, I'll say Baiae in Italy given its rarity. The sites above ground were simply luxurious, and the sites underwater (we *scuba dived!*) were even more magical while swimming above them surrounded by fish. But my favorite museum goes to Mérida. It was massive, beautifully constructed, and had some of the best mosaics I have ever seen.

Grace: My favorite archaeological site was Pompeii. Just before the trip I took a class about the archaeology of Pompeii (and Herculaneum and Stabiae, which unfortunately didn't fit into our itinerary), so it was wonderful to visit the city again with all the new knowledge I gained in the course. Also, with this being my third visit to the site, the city felt like a familiar environment to me despite its antiquity, which was a nice surprise. As for my favorite museum, I have to say Palazzo Massimo because of the artifacts it houses. It has the garden frescoes from the imperial family's villa at Prima Porta, which I did my Centro site report on and so will always be exceptionally fond of. But what really captures my heart are the two Roman calendars that are there!

What was your favorite non-Classical site/activity?

Zoë: Can I say driving again? Actually I'll say the beach at Ostia. We were so tired and hot from walking around Ostia Antica in the heat with very little shade, so when we got to the beach we basically ran and collapsed into the water. It was the most euphoric moment and very healing. That was also the first time we went to the beach after Portugal, so it felt like a win.

Grace: If returning to the Centro and walking around Monteverde (the neighborhood it's located in) counts as a 'non-Classical activity,' then that was my favorite. It felt, in a way, like coming home.

What did you learn from this trip?

Zoë: Besides the pivotal role of lamps in the ancient world? I definitely learned that not much, ultimately, has changed. Not the important things, at least. We actually repeated this exact line at almost every site we visited—jokingly, of course. But it was funny because it's true. As our guide at Évora taught us, the beauty of learning history is that you find out human beings share some simple, weighty truths, and that history—and dare I say, life—is meaningful because of them.

Grace: While I did learn many new facts that I found absolutely fascinating, the most important lesson I learned from the trip is, perhaps ironically, that there is always more to learn. Every site and museum had something new to teach us, from the peculiarities of Roman houses in the province of Hispania to the role of bees in Delphi to the machinery behind the Greeks' calculations of the lunar and solar calendars. No matter how much I read about the ancient world or travel through it, there will forever be a new detail for me to discover, which I find exciting and delightful.

If you could describe the trip in one word, what would it be?

Zoë: Imaginative. When Grace and I talked about this question beforehand, we both said "immersive" at the same time—only half-joking (*submersive* was the next joke, thanks to our scuba diving excursion)—so I thought I'd pick a different word. I feel like on this trip more than others I've taken, especially with our blog, we tried to imagine each site as it was in the ancient world. We tried to imagine the traveling, the buildings, the roads, the people, and everything in between. And even though at times it felt so close as to touch and at others very far away, trying to imagine how it all used to be led to some surprising and interesting revelations that have completely changed my perspective on history.

Grace: 'Immersive' does capture the trip perfectly, but like Zoë I have another word: moving. And I mean 'moving' in more than one sense. First of all, we were always on the move, between sites and museums and cities and countries. When I think back on this trip I will always remember how tired my legs were at the end of every day, which reflected the enormous amount of energy and excitement that we gave to each of our experiences. Second, this trip moved me in a temporal sense. As Zoë's choice of 'imaginative' captures, we were constantly attempting to place ourselves into the perspectives of the ancient people who actually inhabited and used these sites and artifacts. I felt that as the trip progressed I became better and better at moving myself into the ancient world. Finally, this trip was emotionally moving for me. I freely admit that the sites we saw often made me teary-eyed from their majesty, and as I am currently at a major turning-point in my life, this trip was transformative, empowering, and healing for me.

Finally, what would be your ideal next journey if you had the means?

Zoë: Definitely Turkey, Tunisia, and Egypt. Southern Europe is just one part of the much bigger landscape of the Ancient Mediterranean world. If it were possible and within my means, exploring ancient sites like Göbekli Tepe, Hattuşa, Troy, Ephesus, Carthage, Memphis, Thebes, and Alexandria and getting a sense of the vastness and wealth of these ancient empires would be really inspiring. Once I realized that the empires of the Hittites and Egyptians were as old to the ancient Romans and Greeks as the latter are to us, it was hard to ignore their ancient significance and mythological depth.

Grace: I'd like to travel through more of the Roman provinces. One thing I really loved about this trip was visiting Portugal and Spain and learning about their pre-Roman indigenous communities through artifacts and archaeological sites. I have a family connection to England, so it would be especially meaningful to me to travel there and see the Roman ruins in places like York as well as learn about the indigenous peoples. However, like Zoë, I also hope to travel all over, from Nîmes to Alexandria to Istanbul, to name just a few ideal destinations.

§

To end this collection of essays, a huge thank you to everyone who followed our journey, whether on social media or the blog or both, and if you are reading this book, thank you for supporting our project! It was such a fun and immersive journey, but sharing all that we experienced and learned with others made it even more meaningful. We hope to return one day for another ancient empire trip...

Until then, *adeus, adiós, arrivederci,* & αντίο!

ABOUT THE AUTHORS

Grace DeAngelis (left) graduated from Northwestern University in 2023 with a bachelor's degree in Classics, concentrating in Greek and Latin. She studied abroad at the Intercollegiate Center for Classical Studies in Rome during the 2021 fall semester, where she met Zoë! Having written a senior thesis about the lunar calendar and pregnancy in Ovid's *Fasti*, Grace is especially fascinated by the Roman calendar and conceptions of time in antiquity. Other interests include Latin poetry, historiography, mythical narratives, and aetiology. Grace has continued her education as a Ph.D. student in the Classics department at Princeton University. To contact her, please email gdeangelis@princeton.edu.

Zoë Tavares Bennett (right) graduated from Williams College in 2023 with a degree in Classics, specializing in Greek and Latin. Zoë also attended the Intercollegiate Center for Classical Studies in Rome during Fall 2021. She will continue her ancient language study at UCLA's Proto-Indo-European Studies PhD program, with research interests in Homeric Greek & Sanskrit. Her paper "The Art of Thinking in Sapphic Greek: Translation, Language, & Environment" has been published by Stanford's Undergraduate Journal for Classical Studies, *Aisthesis*. She has also published an ancient historical novel on the rise of Emperor Augustus, *The Sun of God*, as well as an ancient Mediterranean-inspired fantasy trilogy, *The Realm of Emmeson*, available on Amazon. For more information, visit her author's website, www.zoetavaresbennett.com.

www.ingramcontent.com/pod-product-compliance
Lightning Source LLC
Chambersburg PA
CBHW040440150626

46551CB00026B/463